Paddling the Yukon River and its Tributaries

A Guide to
Paddling Across Alaska and the Yukon Territory
on the
Yukon, Tanana, Porcupine, and Koyukuk Rivers
Plus the Kuskokwim River

By Dan Maclean

Maps by Colleen Shannon and Dan Maclean

PO Box 221974 Anchorage, Alaska 99522-1974
books@publicationconsultants.com—www.publicationconsultants.com

ISBN 1-59433-027-1

Library of Congress Catalog Card Number: 2005900639

Backcover map and maps introducing each river are ©2003, Government
of Canada with permission from Natural Resources Canada. Base data for
the section maps is used by permission of the United States Geological Survey
under their Fair Use Agreement. These particular presentations are ©2005
Dan Maclean. Historical images are used by permission of the Anchorage
Museum of History and Art, and the Alaska State Library. River flow graphs
are used with permission from: Brabets, Timothy and all. *Environmental
and Hydrologic Overview of the Yukon River Basin, Alaska and Canada*,
U.S. Geological Survey, Water Resources Investigations Report 99-4204,
Anchorage, AK, 2000.

Manufactured in the United States of America.

Acknowledgments

Although I paddled these rivers and wrote this guide alone, I could not have done any of it without help. Nearly six years have elapsed from paddling the first river to binding these pages, and many, many people have generously stepped forward along the way. What started out as a solo paddle has turned into a group project.

While canoeing the Yukon River, Chris and Kelly Kane, Kirsten Hoppe, Alan Block, Jessica Cochran and the APRN staff either took care of my dog, mailed food, lent gear, or helped share the trip.

The second time doing anything, you always seem to make the most mistakes. On the Koyukuk River, I was in particular need of help. Kristiann Rutzler, Jessica Cochran, Nathan Pannkuk, Kirsten Hoppe, and Teresa Bakker supplied it. Plus, thanks to the guy who gave me a skiff ride from Koyukuk to Galena, and the people who put me up there, whose names I have now forgotten, but not how they gave a hand.

Kristiann Rutzler and Jivan Dhaliwal drove the Dempster Highway with me, arriving at Eagle River, leading to the Porcupine River. Jessica Cochran and Nathan Pannkuk watched Rheingold. And thanks to the guy from Old Crow who met a stranger and invited me into his home for the Gathering, broadening my horizons.

On the Tanana, Kristiann Rutzler and the whole Chilkoot Pass crew helped me arrive. Glenda Richard provided a place to land in Fairbanks.

It was great seeing John Hoppe on the Kuskokwim River. And, of course, couldn't of done it without Kristiann.

Sarah Kirk and Shannon Gramse, editors of the poetry journal Ice-Floe, kindly read early drafts of this—and other—manuscripts. This is a guidebook, and certainly not poetry. But it is a relief to hear positive criticism after laboring alone on a project for so long.

Jac Summers, Brian Shumaker, Garth Hitchings, Gabriel Spitzer, and Kristiann Rutzler all pitched in on the scribbling, too.

The maps and cover would have been chicken scratch without the hard work, skill, and persistence of Colleen Shannon of Bus11 Design. They are a fundamental part of this book. Colleen repeatedly developed creative ideas, and worked late almost every weekend in the winter of 2005. Thanks.

Shana Sheehy of the Alaska Teen Media Institute has kindly helped spread the word of this book.

And I couldn't do anything at all without Kristiann Rutzler. Plus the clan Maclean, the old DC crew, and my now departed friend Rheingold.

Table of Contents

Maps

Introduction

The five rivers detailed in *Paddling the Yukon River and its Tributaries*—the Yukon, Kuskokwim, Porcupine, Tanana, and Koyukuk—are the five longest rivers in Alaska, extending into the Yukon Territory. Their combined 4,000 miles of channel flow through the last large wilderness in North America.

Canoeing on the Tanana River toward Cathedral Rapids. The Alaska Range towers over the water and the first snows of the year are just dusting the peaks. Paddling in the fall-such as early September-is a gorgeous time of year to see Alaska. The tundra is turning red, the birches and poplars are turning yellow, and there are almost no bugs.

This guide approaches these rivers like a through-hiker on the Appalachian or Pacific Crest Trails, but in a boat and following a natural trail. The through-paddler floats the intersection of geology, gravity, and weather that creates a clear path, many bug-free camping spots, and the buoyancy to carry large loads of food between distant resupply points.

The five rivers are only sparsely modified by people. There are two small dams on the Yukon above Whitehorse; all other water is free flowing. The rivers hardly rise when the sky pours inches of rain on a swampy drainage or may swell three feet overnight if it drizzles on impermeable permafrost. Salmon surge upriver in pulses to spawn without outside help. Bears troll the banks for spawned-out fish. Moose swim to the islands to calve, their new-born protected from predatory bears by the river moat. Many residents in villages along the banks live a subsistence lifestyle.

This is country that no longer exists in the Lower 48 states or in southern Canada. You do not need a permit to be here. You can discover your own camp spot on an island in the middle of endless forests, hills, and swamps, and within a season after paddling on, even your footprints are erased from the sand. There are so few people, chatting away the afternoon with a stranger over a thermos of coffee will linger in your mind for years.

This guidebook strives to maintain a sense of adventure and discovery, while still providing enough information for a safe and comfortable trip. A general introduction focuses on preventing mistakes that might arise from misconceptions about the Bush. Then, each river is introduced with a map and an overall planning section, thoroughly discussing required skills, logistics, gear, and travel techniques specific to that ribbon of water, emphasizing independence and a limited budget. The river is then broken down into sections which are possible to cover as shorter trips. Within these segment descriptions are maps and Significant Points comments, highlighting features including resupply points, camping tips, historical stories, and possible hazards.

This book will not hold your hand around every river bend. It assumes familiarity with paddling and outdoor living. If

A rainbow makes a Porcupine River camp that much more comfortable. This sandy island is almost at the end of the Flats, about twenty miles above the village of Fort Yukon.

you are interested in history—natural or human—excellent books on these subjects are listed in the bibliography. Some guides to the Yukon headwaters are more detailed than this one and *Paddling the*

Yukon River and its Tributaries points them out where appropriate. But no book has ever taken this comprehensive, headwaters-to-delta approach to floating these rivers. If you read closely, plan thoroughly, and paddle conservatively, you should have a safe trip with a trunk full of memories to savor for a long lifetime.

And so enjoy dreaming about, planning for, and then paddling these rivers. Canoeing them has been one of the highlights of my life; may it be one of the highlights of yours as well.

Long Distance Paddling in the North

These five rivers cover more than 4,000 miles of arctic, subarctic, and boreal country. No matter how varied the terrain these diverse rivers drain, there are many skills common to paddling each one comfortably and safely. This section discusses them in detail.

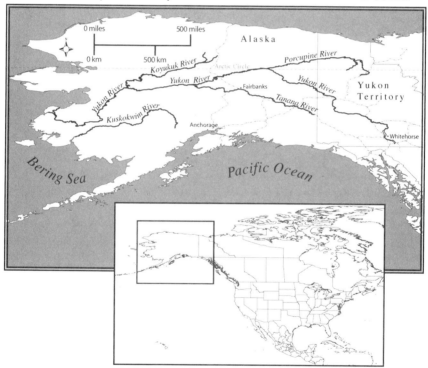

Experience and Preparation

If you can point a boat in the direction you want to travel and then follow through on that path, you have the technical skills necessary to paddle any of these rivers. There are a few short rapids on the Yukon, and some sections of the Tanana and upper Kuskokwim are so heavily braided they place a premium on route-picking skills, but the water is mostly smooth and has more in common with a lake than with a river.

That does not mean anyone should go. All these trips require judgment, wilderness experience, and a positive mental attitude. If you get into any sort of trouble, there will be no one around to help you—cell phones usually do not work and many rivers are rarely traveled. If you decide midtrip that floating down a river through God's country is not for you, there are very few places to pull out, and these opportunities become increasingly rare and difficult the farther you get from a road crossing. Food planning (discussed in later sections) over a long distance is also an essential skill. And you must have the mental self-discipline to motivate yourself to cover a set distance every day. The best experiences for acquiring these skills are not paddling rapids on weekends, traipsing through crowded national parks, or camping with organizations, but independent boating or even hiking for long distances and periods of time, preferably in remote, unregulated country.

One of the better ways to acquire these skills is to paddle shorter sections of these rivers before tackling a complete headwaters-to-delta trip. The upper Yukon River from Whitehorse to Dawson is a two-week paddle. There are many services along the way for visitors, and a number of road crossings make shorter trips possible if necessary. Plus, this section of the Yukon is among the most scenic stretches of water anywhere on earth. The upper Tanana River is also an excellent beginner's river for the long-distance paddler. It parallels or frequently crosses highways for the majority of its flow; a short, flat section such as Northway Junction to Tanacross or George Lake Lodge over a long weekend is a good trip to learn the basics of multiday paddling. Perhaps a number of trips on short sections will help you decide if a two-month paddle is something you want to commit to.

Hiking trips such as completing the Pacific Crest Trail, the Appalachian Trail, the John Muir Trail, the Long Trail or something similar also provide an excellent background for long floats. Although you're obviously walking on these trails and not paddling, they do teach you the state of mind necessary to travel a set distance each day, food planning over long periods of time, and basic map reading. These skills are more likely to help you safely reach the delta than the ability to pirouette a boat through whitewater.

Lastly, aside from a long-distance trip background, the paddler must have more than enough time to do the trip. You can be just 10 miles from the end of a month-long journey, but if the wind picks up, the safest way to travel is sitting inside a pitched tent, waiting the weather out. One of the most common causes of accidents is pushing ahead through rough weather to return at a specific time.

Paddling Partners

A partner has more effect on the trip than any piece of equipment. This discussion is probably as futile as marriage advice—and as unwelcome. But the subject is such an important component of any trip that is has to be addressed.

Compatible personalities are more important than paddling experience. The group will be spending some serious quality time together. Many married couples paddle these rivers, and that can expand the experience in many ways. Not only can the bond between you grow stronger, but villagers will be more open and friendly to a couple than they will be to two guys or to a single person. Some parts of these rivers are even suitable for families with children.

Besides being dangerous and lonely, traveling alone makes it hard to take pictures of people. The timer went off a little sooner than expected for this shot.

It can be a good idea for two people to travel in two different boats. This way, you can have some separation during the day while still enjoying the advantages of each other's company in camp at night. Plus, you have the safety of two boats in case one boat has problems.

As anyone who has planned a long trip probably knows, though, partners can be enthusiastic and eager up until it's time to go, at which point they discover other priorities. Frequently, the only way to do long trips is to go alone.

Traveling solo is not recommended.

Now that the legal disclaimer is out of the way, I paddled all these rivers by myself. It works for me. It is not for everybody. Expect to go up to two weeks without talking to someone else. This is a long time without conversation, so be sure you are experienced at keeping yourself entertained. If not, you will go through a rough patch as you learn. Besides guaranteed loneliness, traveling alone can also be dangerous. Be much more cautious than usual. Pull over and camp at the first sign of rough weather. Bring more than enough warm, dry clothes. If there are fresh bear tracks on a gravel bar, keep pushing on into the evening until you find a camp without fresh sign.

You will also have to develop a sixth sense about leaving the boat and gear unattended on village beaches to make a phone call or buy groceries. Vandalism and theft, while rare, have occurred over the years. When traveling alone, it helps to time your arrival at the community in the morning, when fewer people are wandering around.

You are unlikely to meet another paddler on the water who wants to travel with you, except maybe on the Yukon and Porcupine Rivers.

Boat Type

Boat selection is second only to choice of paddling partner in affecting the character of your trip. As in partner choice, there are no clear right or wrong boats; however, rafts are strongly discouraged. Each option has its own merits and faults.

Canoes can carry lots of gear, are comfortable to sit in eight to ten hours a day, day in day out, are relatively cheap, and even make excellent tents flipped over in high winds. It is possible to carry more than a month's food in a canoe, and this is their primary practical advantage. You don't have to worry about resupplying frequently and whatever time is lost battling wind can be made up by not having to stop in villages to restock. Additionally, since a full food bag is a major component of a safe journey, canoes can be safer boats than sea kayaks, provided you are cautious enough to get off the river quickly when the wind picks up. Plus, the extra room in a canoe lets you shift and stretch your legs and body position, a tremendous comfort on a long trip. If you do decide to canoe, choose a boat with a deep keel to help hold a track in the wind. Most recreational canoes have flat bottoms to easily maneuver on small creeks and rivers, but these flat water rivers have turning room to spare.

Sea kayaks slice through wind and waves more easily than canoes. The majority of paddlers on big rivers such as the Yukon and Kuskokwim find this overcomes the primary disadvantages of kayaks: small carrying capacity, cramped seating, and an awkward entry into the cockpit. Plus, you can use the foot rudder to drift hands-free down the river, munching snacks, sipping morning coffee, and staring off into space, all while steering.

Packable kayaks and canoes are excellent boats to transport on small planes, in a heavy backpack, or even by mail. On water, they leave a lot to be desired. They are difficult to beach, have a relatively small carrying capacity, and get blown off course in the wind more easily than their hard-shell counterparts. They must be unloaded every night and firmly anchored within hearing distance of the tent since porcupines have been known to chew the wooden frames. People do occasionally use them to float these rivers, but aside from making it easy to fly out from even the smallest village, they have no real practical advantages while floating.

I have heard of people using seagoing rowboats. These craft look like sea kayaks, but the paddler sits on top of the hull and strokes backward with two oars. Apparently they just glide through head-winds and waves and have the further advantage of lockable cargo compartments that approach the capacity of a canoe. Before I went out and plunked down money on a sea kayak, I would test and seriously consider this unusual form of boat.

Under very few circumstances would I recommend traveling in any form of raft. Rafts put you at the mercy of the current, they cannot travel in wind, and locals are very suspicious of people traveling on them. People on rafts are usually more than a little nuts and villagers will call you "Huck Finn" and they don't mean it as a compliment. The two worst things about rafts are you cannot travel when it is windy, so you can be pinned in one spot for days on end, and they can be difficult to eddy out on swift rivers.

Practical considerations aside, the choice of boat boils down to the type of boat you are most comfortable and familiar with. You two are going to be spending some time together, and it helps if you get along.

Budgeting

The amount of money you spend varies according to which river you choose, how you approach the beginning and end of the trip, your assorted equipment choices, and whether or not you buy a boat just for one trip. The emphasis of this guidebook is on doing this as cheaply as possible, and the least expensive alternatives are clearly laid out. For a ball park figure, though, count on spending around one thousand dollars per month of paddling, assuming you start and finish in a transportation hub city such as Anchorage, Fairbanks, or Whitehorse. Then, whatever amount of money you plan to spend, double it.

Keeping in Touch

Cellphones do not work on any of these rivers, except on short portions of the Yukon, Tanana, and Kuskokwim.

You should telephone regularly to a responsible, caring person off the river who is keeping track of your progress. Frequently, this means calling from a landline in a village. It is difficult to balance the safety of calling in at a set time and avoiding turning the trip into a perpetual slog to the next phone to keep that person from calling the cops. Or worse, paddling through rough water to reach a phone when the prudent paddler is camping on a gravel bar, waiting out the weather. What seems to work best is to set a window of time to expect a call, with a very specific date after that window when your minder calls the Alaska State Troopers or the Royal Canadian Mounted Police. At every call, clearly name the village you're in, change the next call window and the "call-the-cops date," making sure that all information is written down. Even as remote as these rivers are, it is possible to reach a public telephone weekly (with the exception of remote stretches of the Porcupine).

Pay phones are uncommon in smaller villages. Instead, all City Offices have public-use lines that allow calling card or prepaid phone card calls. (Call charges from the Bush are exorbitant, so the investment in a prepaid card is well worth it). The City Office building is almost always unmarked, so just ask around to find it. Often, there is only one telephone line for the whole building, so plan to keep your phone time short and to the point. Expect people to listen to your conversation. And, of course, say thanks when you are done.

If you feel the need for constant and private telephone contact, a satellite telephone, while expensive, works consistently.

Weather and Light

The old New England saying, "If you don't like the weather, wait fifteen minutes," is true in Alaska and the Yukon, too. It can snow, erupt into a thunderstorm, and/or be a 90-degree scorcher all in the same day. Having said that, there are some general weather patterns.

Interior Alaska and Yukon weather is dry, continental weather that tends to change quickly—think of the northern Rocky Mountains in the Lower 48 and Canada. As soon as the weather turns to summer, usually in the beginning of June, it turns quite hot, sunny, and relatively dry. When it does rain in the Interior, it gets chilly. And even in the middle of July snowflakes are not unheard of.

Closer to the ocean, the air becomes cooler and wetter. Storms don't erupt as suddenly as in the Interior, but they tend to last longer and are much more violent.

Late July and August are typically rainy and in the 40s or 50s. Fall starts around the end of August or the beginning of September, with winter following rapidly. Floating these rivers in late September is pushing your luck.

The term "land of the midnight sun" is a cliché because it is true. Although the sun technically sets, or lowers to a certain angle on the horizon, it doesn't get entirely dark in the summer. Even as far south as Whitehorse, there is just a deep twilight around two or three in the morning in June and July. If you are not used to the light, it might take a few days before you fully adjust to the idea of not telling time by how light or dark it is and falling asleep when it's sunny. Most people find all the light invigorating. Regardless, you don't need to worry about packing a flashlight in midsummer.

A squall on the Porcupine River shows a range of possible July weather: cold rain and wind, quickly followed by still air and sun.

Stuff

Flipping through outdoor gear catalogues, you would begin to think that you can't leave the climate-conditioned comfort of home without a $1,000 arrangement of petrochemical fibers armoring your body against storms or a set of collapsible titanium chopsticks to nosh some grub. You don't need all that junk. Although boats easily carry lots of gear, it pays to keep the number of bags to a minimum—a month into the trip, when you've packed and unpacked the boat close to 60 times, reducing the number of trips between camp and the boat begins to take on a whole new importance. Out of necessity, you become as organized as a factory manager.

The gear listed on page 16 fits comfortably in a 16-foot canoe with one person. Different boat types vary in their capacity and organization. Experiment with packing the boat before leaving, making sure it has extra space to handle lots of food and the load is balanced with the center of gravity low and in the middle. No matter if the trip will be two weeks or two and a half months, you should pack the same amount and type of gear; you should be prepared for the full spectrum

Sleeping Dry Bag

- Sleeping bag
- Sleeping pad
- Journal, pen, and book. (These items are stored in a separate small dry bag within the larger sleeping dry bag because the sleeping bag is frequently wet.)

Clothing Dry Bag

- Paperback library
- Maps for upcoming and previously traveled country
- Nylon jacket with fleece lining (Some people call it a squall jacket.)
- Thick wool sweater
- 2 pairs expedition-weight polyester long johns (They stay warm when wet.)
- 1 pair nylon shorts
- 1 pair Carhartt carpenter pants (Bugs can't bite through them.)
- 1 wool shirt
- Thick wool hat
- Neoprene gloves
- 4 pairs of socks—2 heavy, 2 light
- Long-sleeve permanent press shirt or any lightweight shirt that cuts down on sunburn and dries quickly.
- Xtra-Tufs
- Tent repair kit
- Boat body repair kit
- Dry-bag repair kit
- Duct tape
- Extra rope
- Spare tarp (A very handy item for dumping all your gear on the beach when doing bag cleaning and reorganizing or setting the tent up underneath when it's pouring rain.)

Food Dry Bag

All food except lunch is kept in an oversized dry bag along with:
- Gasoline stove (Although white gas is available in most villages, gasoline is available in every one.)
- Aluminum pot
- Spoon
- Leatherman
- Spices
- Unscented soap

Waterproof Gun Case

- 12-gauge shotgun and 10 slugs
- Gun-cleaning kit
- 1 can bear repellent pepper spray

Day-use Dry Bag

- Lunch
- Camera (Carry two, since sand tends to get in the works.)
- Film
- Bug dope and headnet
- Address book and wallet
- Toilet paper
- Water filter
- Sunglasses
- Sun block
- Leatherman (Take two. They tend to get left behind.)
- First-aid kit

Loose Gear

- 2 paddles per person, 1 spare lashed to the boat
- 2 life jackets per person (One worn, one used as a kneepad in rough water. They make excellent pillows.)
- 1 gallon white gas
- Tent and ground cloth

Net Bag 1

- Water jugs
- Thermos
- Coffee cup

Net Bag 2

- Commercial-fishing-quality rain suit

Waterproof Map Case

of conditions. The only gear that should vary with trip length is food and the number of times you resupply it.

All gear is packed in dry bags except the tent, which is frequently wet with dew or rain, and your rain suit, gallon can of white gas, and water bottles, which are packed in easily accessible net bags. All bags are securely tied to the boat.

Loading a canoe takes experience. The large bag toward the bow is the food bag, the single heaviest item. This balances the solo paddler weight to the stern. Most other gear is arranged according to how frequently it needs to be used while keeping the boat balanced. Rain gear is in a net bag directly in front of the paddler. Lunch and camera is in the bag near the stern. The map case is tied to the seat. Make sure to tie all gear to the boat in case it flips. Experiment to find a system that works for you before leaving on a long trip. As a further note, this is a two-person canoe paddled alone. Sitting in the bow seat and paddling the boat backward makes the boat considerably easier to handle.

I have used every item on this list at least once, with the exception of the boat patch kit, which I carry anyway. Some items are more useful than others and deserve a full explanation.

The commercial-fishing-quality rainsuit—a one piece jacket-and-hood combination plus bib pants with suspenders—keeps you dry even when it is raining sideways near the Bering Sea or wetly snowing north of the Arctic Circle in July. It is like walking around in a truly waterproof tent. Goretex rainwear, ponchos, and so forth just don't cut it in those conditions.

Xtra-Tuf boots also make an oversized contribution to paddler happiness. The boots with the funny name are neoprene and worn, again, by commercial fishermen. They are as comfortable as a pair of sneakers, but keep your feet as dry and clean as a pair of rubber boots. I buy them slightly too large to wear two pairs of socks and tuck my pants inside them. The only caveat about rubber boots is to remove them before heading into rough water. If you capsize, they can fill with silt, quickly dragging you to the bottom. I wear Xtra-Tufs despite this remote danger because of the more immediate prospect of hypothermia from wet feet.

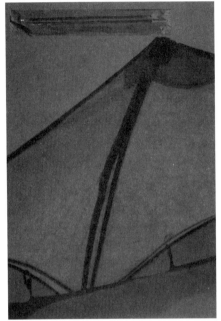

The last item that truly makes an overwhelming contribution to your comfort and safety is a sleeping bag. Take one that is polyester filled and comfort-rated to around 0 or –10 degrees Fahrenheit. This might seem excessively warm for summer. It is not. Even when you're thoroughly soaked and sitting in a puddle, the bag will be comfortable, as long as you don't mind sleeping in what feels like a wet suit.

There aren't too many outdoor gear stores along these rivers. If something breaks or is lost, you have to make do. A stove part and a tarp pole are modified to support the body of the tent. And a whittled willow stick supports the tarp. All because I lost one tent pole section. A word from the wise: check camp each morning to make sure you aren't leaving anything behind.

Carry two to three times the normal number of tent stakes—double or triple staking in an X pattern helps anchor the tent to soft sand in the wind. Nothing wears out a tent faster than sand. Leave your boots outside, folding over the tops so rain can't fill them. Be sure to shake the grit out of the tent every morning. Even with this constant care, zipper pulls will quickly wear out and the waterproof coating will wear off. Bring recoating spray if you will be paddling for more than six weeks.

Which brings up repair kits. The assemblages of flimsy junk sold in most outdoor stores are not adequate to the task. Bring industrial-quality adhesive, scraps of sandpaper, and junked vinyl to repair dry bags, rainsuits, and rubber boots. (If you have to glue a patch to your food dry bag, air the bag out in the evenings to avoid infusing food with acetone). Bring metal replacement zipper pulls, thick nylon thread with strong needles, and seam sealer to repair tents and sleeping bags. Bring O-rings to repair stoves and fuel bottles.

A Leatherman is the most compact and versatile repair kit of all. With its many tools, you can whittle a new tent pole and file an extra piece of stove to fit in the pole grommet if need be. There are almost no sporting good stores once you start paddling these rivers; you have to be self-sufficient and creative.

Make sure all gear is in excellent shape before leaving. If something looks like it is getting worn out at the beginning of the trip, count on it breaking at the worst possible moment.

Maps

United States Geological Survey (USGS) and Natural Resources Canada (NRCanada) 1: 250,000 scale maps are the best way to navigate. Most of these maps were made in the 1950s and have been only partially and sporadically updated since then. The channels and islands have changed in some places. Many villages listed on the maps no longer exist, are just fish camps, or have been moved to avoid flooding (all existing villages are named in the upcoming Rest and Resupply Points sections of individual rivers). Despite these shortcomings, the maps are more than accurate enough for navigation and planning. They are available from the USGS from their website www.usgs.gov .

Canadian maps are sold only through dealers and are available over the Internet from retailers worldwide. For general Canadian topographic map questions and a complete list of map dealers, contact Natural Resources Canada directly at:

Policy and Product Promotion Office
Centre for Topographic Information
Natural Resources Canada 711-615 Booth Street
Ottawa, Ontario, Canada
K1A 0E9
1-800-465-6277
topo.maps@NRCan.gc.ca
http://maps.NRCan.gc.ca

Many maps are now available in electronic formats. These are all based on USGS or NRCanada data. Never rely solely on electronic maps or GPS units. Sand and rain quickly destroy electronics. The money spent on large paper maps is well spent since they don't break easily. Plus, you get a better feeling of the overall country and it is easier to navigate by sight from a large piece of paper.

Food

There are three main ways of stocking up on food in Bush Alaska. The first is to take a fully stocked pantry from the start. The second is to buy food at village stores. The third is to mail packages to villages along the way. All these methods have advantages and disadvantages, and most people will wind up using some combination of the three.

Carrying food from the beginning is easy and largely self-explanatory. The descriptions of the individual rivers list the best places to stock up at the headwaters. The section following this one discusses the making of the "meal of the trip" from food that is readily available in grocery stores and doesn't rot. Most boats don't have enough capacity to carry food for more than a month, so if it will be a long journey, bring enough spices, vitamins, and other small, hard to find items to last the entire trip.

Mailed food packages provide the cheapest and most varied grub since you can shop in a large city, but it is also the most unreliable and complicated way to resupply. It works best when packages are sent from a hub Alaska post office, such as Anchorage or Fairbanks, to an Alaska village; or, in the Yukon Territory, from Whitehorse to a Canadian Bush village. When resupplying this way, I leave stamped packages with responsible friends, who agree to mail them at set times, using the address form:

> Paddler Name
> "General Delivery"
> Town, State, Zip Code

I call the friends a week before arriving where the packages will be sent—always at a different time than originally planned—at which point they mail the food. It usually takes two to three days for the package to travel from the hub to the Bush, where general-delivery packages are held for ten days. You have to have a driver's license or passport for identification to pick up general-delivery packages. This system provides a flexible window of time to pick up the food. Mailing to the Bush does not work well from the South-48, the provinces, or across the international border—delivery time is wildly inconsistent. A letter between those two places can take anywhere from one day to three months. Just like rafting, mailing food from the South-48 or provinces to the Bush is categorically not recommended.

It is possible to eat by restocking along the way, with a few cautions in mind. Village stores are open only for limited hours and generally carry only a sparse selection of goods by city grocery standards. They reliably stock the essentials: Spam, canned chili, ramen noodles, Pilot Bread (hardtack crackers), peanut butter, and sugar in all its lovely forms.

Fruits and vegetables are uncommon, usually not terribly fresh, and are always expensive—count on paying nearly $2 an apple in smaller villages. And, although people appreciate you spending a little money to help out the local economy, you should refrain from stocking up on items and buying the store out. Villagers have few shopping alternatives and restocking can be slow. In some relatively large villages, stores have a broad, frequently restocked selection; these communities are highlighted in each river's description.

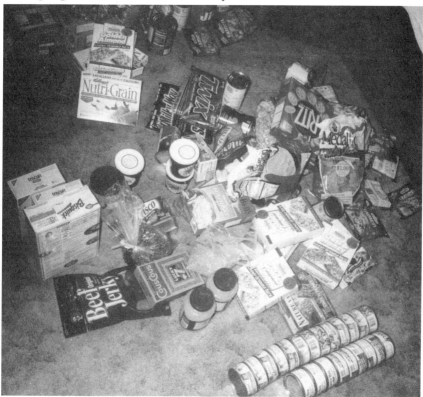

Two months worth of food sprawls across the living room floor, waiting to be boxed and addressed for mailing. You will get curious questions from the clerk at the grocery store when you check out with this much food.

As a last food note, many people seem to be under the impression that it is possible to live off the land while floating down the river by fishing, hunting, and berry picking. *Do not count on the river to provide food.* Most berries do not ripen until August and they grow on land away from the riverbank. Fishing and hunting require separate licenses in Canada and Alaska. These activities are strictly regulated and rigorously enforced by both governments. Most hunting is banned in the summer. Fishing can be unreliable—salmon fishing particularly so. Salmon migrate up the river in pulses and it takes time and experience to learn when the fish are running. Most fishing on these muddy rivers is done with nets or fish wheels. Salmon do not feed once they enter freshwater and the river is muddy and wide, so the combined odds of a salmon striking your lure are low. Plus, locals already take almost all the best fishing spots and some season openings are open only to village residents.

All that said, fishing is a fine way to unexpectedly replace your Meal of the Trip. With a rod, you can work the clear feeder streams, nailing pike, grayling, trout, and sheefish so frequently you will probably never want to eat fish again. Just don't count on it.

Meal of the Trip

It takes a little experience to come up with a cheap, nutritious, and filling diet that doesn't rot. Notice that taste isn't the primary consideration. I used to hate the bland, dry taste of Pilot Bread—hardtack crackers that never go bad since they are made stale. But, after associating

Ah, the many possibilities of Meal of the Trip. Here are just a few: ramen, black bean soup, and canned chicken; mac and cheese and chicken; couscous, lentils, and turkey. It tastes good normally and great when you're cold and hungry. As a last note, driftwood makes a fantastic windscreen for your stove. Another word from the wise: paddle blades don't. (And a further lesson: a backup paddle really is useful).

Pilot Bread with the comforting feeling of a full belly on river trips, I now even eat it at home sometimes. Taste comes with time.

For breakfast, I usually eat cheese and Pilot Bread, then peanut butter and Pilot Bread for lunch, apples, granola bars, and candy for snacks, and the Meal of the Trip for supper. I do my best to get fresh apples in villages, but it is not always possible to find them. To stay healthy, substitute dried or canned fruit when fresh is not available. The Meal of the Trip is more of a concept than a specific group of ingredients. The recipe mixes one ingredient from each column to arrive at a one-pot stew that cooks quickly, easily, and fills you up. It is easy to make variations, so just consider this a rough guide.

Starch	Protein	Protein & Fat	Spices
Ramen Noodles	Red Lentils	Canned Chicken	Cajun
Couscous	Black Bean Soup Mix	Canned Turkey	Curry
Instant Rice	Lentil Soup Mix	Canned Ham	Vegetable Soup Mix
Dried Ravioli		Fresh Fish	Salt & garlic
		Tofu & Oil	

Canned food is great on river trips—not only doesn't it rot, but, provided it is packed low and in the center of the boat, also makes great stabilizing ballast.

Water

The water from any of these five rivers is probably okay to drink without treatment on most stretches. The hard part is telling where those stretches are. So, treating the water in some manner is the prudent way to go. There is no real industrial pollution, so you have to worry only about killing things living in the water.

Conventional water filters do not work reliably. Silt plugs them solid after you pump just a few quarts. Instead, the most reliable way to treat river water is to boil the next day's drinking water in the evening and let the grit settle to the bottom of the pot overnight. In the morning, you can carefully pour clear water off the top of the pot, discarding the mud at the bottom. This method of making drinking water has the advantage that it takes very little time and effort, making time for other camp chores or staring off into the distance while the water boils. On the down side, you can't quickly make more water during the day if you unexpectedly need more. You will also burn more fuel and need a larger cooking pot than usual and should plan accordingly.

If the idea of drinking main-stem river water is unappealing, you can load up on clear water from feeder streams during the day and purify it. The downside is the time and effort spent tracking down the clear water. Some of the tributaries you cross to will turn out to be muddy—a waste of paddling effort. And clear feeders do not exist at all in many swampy sections or during high water. Of course, the advantage is you have perfectly clear water that may be further purified by any method you choose, including a filter.

The last possible watering method is to carry very large containers and fill them up from village water supplies. It takes minimal effort to actually get the water, but it means you have to stop frequently. Moreover, many Bush water systems are accessible only during the week, or are locked with a key you have to hunt down. The advantage to watering this way is that you meet people as you search for the village water supply; the disadvantage is you can't restock water if you're stuck on an island in bad weather.

Most people will probably wind up using some combination of the above methods.

Keeping Clean, Dry, and Healthy

The difference between a long paddle and a weekend trip is the difference between living in the wilderness and just visiting. On long trips, washing clothes, washing your body, and drying gear will take up lots of spare time.

All villages have washeterias—combination laundromats, showers, and water wells. In most cases, it is possible to enjoy the luxury of hot water at these places at least once a week. Some paddlers find bathing and washing clothes in the river more convenient. This is fine, but be sure to bring unscented, biodegradable liquid soap (health food stores are good sources of cheap, high quality soap)

Many pictures of people traveling in the wilderness show them in macho action poses. But, if you're living in the wilderness, even mundane tasks have to be attended to, such as brushing your teeth.

and use sand for the heavy scrubbing. If you are in the middle of an unending rainy stretch and can't dry clothes, just wait until the next village with a washeteria. Hanging a line on the inside of the tent to dry clothes nightly stretches how long they can go between washings.

As for bathing yourself, most headwaters are so cold it is comfortable to quickly scrub in the river only on the hottest days. Water tends to warm up farther downriver. In fact, on lower stretches of the Porcupine, the water is so pleasant I saw water skiers without wet suits—one of the strangest things I've ever seen in Alaska.

As long as it doesn't continuously pour rain, it is possible to keep nylon tents and sleeping bags fairly dry. When you first pull into camp, spread them out over willows if they are wet. As long as there is a decent breeze and nothing more than an intermittent drizzle, the gear should be comfortably dry by bedtime.

Lastly, make the effort to walk back into the willows and bury things when going to the bathroom. The very few people who come after you will appreciate it.

Bears, Bugs, and Things that go *Bump* in the Night

Bears, both black and grizzly (or *brown* in Alaskanese), are everywhere in Alaska and the Yukon. Odds are, eventually one will come into camp. This does not have to be a problem if you behave responsibly.

Choosing an ideal camp will occupy a great deal of time and effort. All land below the high water mark on navigable rivers (in other words, every inch in this guide) is public use and open to camping. But some places are better than others. Gravel bars and islands are much less likely to have animal visitors than shore. This picture shows quite a nice mud bar camp on the upper Tanana River. There is firm open ground to cook on; the nearly constant breeze keeps bugs in control. A patch of alders shelters the tent. The canoe is flipped over and securely tied to driftwood for the night.

The most effort should be put into avoiding a bear encounter in the first place. First, choose a campsite away from regular bear travel routes: on an island or gravel bar, well away from the mouths of tributaries, and relatively free of fresh bear tracks. This is not foolproof, but it is the most effective means of reducing a chance encounter. Once you've picked a good camp, keep it clean. Food smells attract and retain bears. Wash the dishes immediately after eating and store them with all other food in airtight containers well away from the tent. Bear bags—hanging food from a tree branch—are usually impractical since most island trees are too short and weak for this purpose. Stor-

Moose will wander into camp sometimes. These two bulls on Eagle River were more curious than most, but they walked on after showing me some stares and macho strutting. Talking at them in a calm, firm tone helped. But I stayed close to the overturned canoe ready to dive under, just in case.

ing food inside an airtight dry bag is adequate; keeping it in a plastic drum is better. Practice good bear hygiene in other respects, too: do not wash with scented soap, do not use citronella, and do not clean, cook, eat, or store fish in camp.

If a bear does come into camp, do not be afraid. Just like dogs, they can sense fear and will make an opportunistic attack if you act submissively. This does not mean that you should be cocky and antagonistic.

Instead, while standing tall, talk firmly to the bear in a deep steady voice, just like you would a bully. Stay away from pitched tents and food bags while doing this. In almost all cases, the bear will wander on in search of easier food. As a last resort, carry pepper spray, and, if you are comfortable with it, a shotgun loaded with deer slugs (handguns are illegal in Canada). You have to take care of yourself.

Moose can also stop by camp. They are fully aware that islands are less traveled by bears, so they flock to them to calve in relative safety in May and early June, and, on smaller rivers, to escape bugs in July and August. Almost all moose will ignore you, but if they do wander into camp, shouting in a firm, but unaggressive tone of voice will cause most to move on. Hunkering down near the boat, ready to dive under it for shelter, while communicating and waiting until they decide to move on is also a good idea.

As an overall rule, animal activity along these major rivers is highest during the early spring and late fall, and lowest during the middle of the summer. River bottoms are the first spots to green up after the thaw, so moose and their predators are attracted to the feed. In the fall, bears frequent the riverbanks, strolling the shore, grazing on spawned-out salmon. In the summer, most animals disperse to the rolling green hills and swamps well away from shore and fewer and fewer fresh tracks will appear in the muddy banks.

Mosquitoes are numerous, vicious, and blood sucking from breakup until the first frost. But almost all of them stay within the protected forest. While the breeze blows on the river and in camp on gravel bars, they should hardly bother you. On rare occasions, though, the breeze dies, and then the bugs swarm. A sealed tent with a fine-mesh bug screen is essential for a comfortable night's sleep. Wear thick, long pants, a nylon jacket, and a mesh mosquito net over your head and face to reduce exposed skin. Armored like this, it's only necessary to smear toxic bug repellent on the back of your hands while you walk around on the gravel bar in the evening.

At least there aren't any snakes.

Locals

A striking variety of people live along these rivers and no quick blurb or even entire book can sum them up. That said, there is a noticeable difference in the way you are treated in towns on the road system and in isolated Bush villages. In a road town, a paddler will most likely be ignored and written off as a tourist with bad hygiene and an excellent sunburn. In the Bush, you are a curiosity. An unobtrusive effort to politely introduce yourself, saying your name, where you're from, and what you're doing there, will go a long way toward making friends in a village. Also, respect private property. In Alaska and the Yukon Territory, all land below the high-water line on navigable bodies of water is open to the public. Above the high-water line it can be a different story. Native corporations have large allotments along rivers and many do not want travelers camping there. There are also a fair number of private fish camps that may make enticing rest stops during nasty weather. Resist the urge. Otherwise, most people are very open, friendly, and glad to talk with a stranger. Just don't take their openness and generosity for granted.

Like anywhere else, though, there is the occasional bad person. These people, though rare, can ruin your trip. Over the years, paddlers have had their boats stolen, thrown in the river, or had their gear otherwise vandalized. The first step to avoid being treated like this is to let people know who you are, as mentioned earlier. The other major step is to avoid camping on village beaches over the weekends. These public places, where most villages let paddlers set up camp, can easily become the targets of some jerk looking to mess with someone who can't get back at them. If you have to wait a couple days for the post office or grocery store to open, camping on a sandbar above the village rather than waiting in town would be a better alternative. You will probably get more restful sleep as well since four-wheelers won't be rumbling by the tent twenty-fours a day.

Another source of trouble is alcohol. Many villages in Alaska and the Yukon have voted to ban it. Respect this rule. Don't use liquor bottles as water jugs or mail food in boxes that once contained alcohol. Bootlegging is a serious crime and it's best not to even have the appearance of possessing alcohol.

Bush villages are quite small, and can be strongly influenced by just a few people. Consequently, each community seems to have a collective personality. Just as with individuals, if you don't quite fit in one spot, keep trying until you find a village that works for you. Although most paddlers set out to these rivers for the wilderness experience, with time your encounters with other people will almost certainly become the most delightful and enduring memories.

Finally

Of course, when your friends hear of your plans to paddle these remote rivers, you will be overrun with advice, very little of it sought, and even less of it accurate or helpful. Hopefully, the advice in this book falls in the minority category. Just in case it does not, let me finish the general introduction by repeating the two pieces of good advice I received before leaving for the first river: red lentil beans cook in five minutes and have fun.

A Few Essential Notes

Confining the twists and turns of a river to the small pages of a book is a problem that any river paddling guide has to overcome. Confining four thousand miles of twists and turns is an epic problem with many facets.

This book principally solves the dilemma by using 1:1,000,000 scale base maps. These maps are more than detailed enough to plan by and generally navigate the country. However, they do not show such fine features as gravel bars and small islands, information that is frequently necessary to plan the day's travel. This guide assumes you will buy USGS or NRCanada 1:250,000 scale maps which do show this level of detail.

But, USGS and NRCanada maps are frequently outdated. In *Paddling the Yukon River and its Tributaries'* maps, the river path is corrected from the official version with a comment where I encountered major changes in the channel. Nevertheless, you should be paying attention to the river and currents, and prepared to do original navigation at all times. If you do not possess this degree of expertise in map and river reading, your skills are insufficient for safe travel on these waters. If a town has disappeared, a mileage mark and comment is frequently included in this book, but the town name is usually not mapped. Contact information will change, businesses will come and go, and towns will expand, contract, or even move since this writing. It is your responsibility to confirm critical information before setting out on the river. This book will eventually be outdated, too.

A GPS grid overlays these maps, easing the transfer of information between the two forms. However, almost all information in the following pages is tied to a clear visual reference, rendering GPS unnecessary.

All mileage figures used in this book are approximate. They are included as a relative measure for clarity in descriptions. The actual miles traveled will vary from person to person and from trip to trip, sometimes significantly. Channels change from year to year, people will take different shortcuts around islands and through sloughs, and, particularly on wide rivers, the distance traveled changes dramatically if you hug the shore or zigzag across the river. Coastal hikers, used to trail measurements in tenths of a mile, will probably be most disconcerted by this degree of uncertainty. You just have to think a little differently.

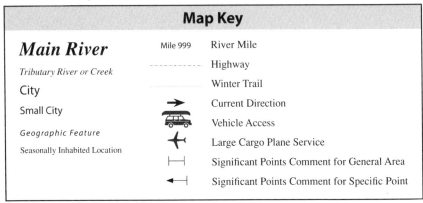

Trip time is also a relative measure. A unit of *one day* presumes paddling steadily for eight hours, including a half-hour break for lunch. Many people find around one to two days off per week is necessary for rest time. This rest time is not included in the section time figures, but is included in the trip time given in the overall river description. This is only an estimate. Actual trip time is affected by many random variables: current reading skill, time spent in towns, water level, current speed, wind direction, and storms. *Always, always, always bring more than enough food to complete the trip.* If the current is sluggish, you will have to take more rest days than usual. Storms will pin you to shore, sometimes for days at a time. You must have the flexibility in food supplies and trip time to account for unexpected delays.

Yukon River

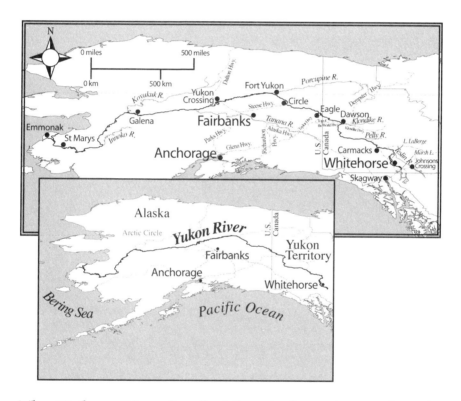

The Yukon River literally defines the far north. It is a through-paddler's dream.

Gathering rain and melting snow across a basin almost half again as large as the state of Texas, the Yukon drains this country through an 1,800 mile-long channel before finally pouring into the Bering Sea. The riverbed is the tenth-longest river in the world and the fourth longest in North America. The headwaters are mountain lakes and glaciers, the central stretch is an enormous swamp, and the lower river has hills on one side and swamp on the other. The Yukon River takes around eight to ten weeks to paddle, but you could do the trip in four months, or paddle the entire river multiple times, and still only experience a sliver of the variety of life along its banks.

Most people immediately think of the Klondike Gold Rush in 1898 when they hear the words *Yukon River*. Around 10,000 stampeding miners floated the headwaters of the largest river in the region to reach gold on the tributary Klondike River. Dawson, the town founded at the junction of the Yukon and Klondike, sat below some of the richest placer gold deposits in the world.

Once the excitement subsided, the Yukon became the region's primary highway, the Mississippi of the North, carrying people and supplies on paddle steamers between villages. This traffic stopped only in the early 1950s, when the Alaska Highway was completed. Today, for 800 miles below the last bridge crossing, the Yukon is still the primary road between villages. Diesel barges travel the lower river, transporting fuel and construction equipment from the road system into the Bush. Skiffs carry people on the watery route between villages.

But the Yukon is more than just a form of transportation; it is also a source of sustenance. Some of the strongest wild salmon runs in the world surge through the channel to spawn. Set nets and fish wheels are anchored to the banks of the lower river, and fish camps dot the shore.

Fewer people live along the Yukon today than 100 years ago and there are many opportunities to paddle in solitude. The lack of roads creates a vast lowland wilderness—rare in these days when most undeveloped land is steep rock and ice. The fertile silt, swamps, and rolling hills attract a menagerie of critters; moose, bears, eagles, and flocks of birds thrive on the rich supply of food in the valley. You can go weeks without seeing another person. Paddling along the Yukon, you can be a free-range cowboy in the best sense of the term.

It is best to break a river and a paddle of this magnitude into sections: Whitehorse to Dawson, Dawson to Circle, the Flats, Yukon Crossing to Galena, and the Run to the Delta. Although planning is the same for any part, each section of the river is geographically and culturally distinct, and it is possible to paddle each as a shorter section or as a segment in a continuous headwaters-to-delta journey.

Yukon River Guide
Planning the Paddle

Where does the Yukon begin and end?

This is actually a rather involved question because the precise beginning and end points of the Yukon are endlessly debatable by reasonable people. The geographic criteria for choosing the beginning of a river should maximize river length and flow by picking the longest and largest tributary stream, which is frequently at the highest elevation. Then add a good dose of opinion.

The highest elevation which eventually drips water into the Bering Sea down the Yukon channel is Llewellyn Glacier, part of the Juneau ice cap, that melts on the southern shore of Atlin Lake, British Columbia. Rick Janowicz, a hydrologist with the Department of Indian Affairs and Northern Development in the Yukon, picked a melt water stream flowing out of the toe of the glacier as the source

1868 map published by the (English) Royal Geographic Society.
(Dan Maclean's collection)

of the Yukon for the 1998 *National Geographic* article, *The Untamed Yukon River*. The editors chose the stream as the source over the glacier—most people imagine flowing water when they think of the beginning of a river.

Long before that moment there had been many debates as to just where the river begins. An 1868 map published by the (English) Royal Geographic Society shows the Yukon beginning only at Fort Yukon, almost 800 miles downriver from Whitehorse. Many later maps declare the beginning to be the junction with the Teslin River, just above Carmacks. The junctions with the White, Stewart, and Pelly Rivers have all also been chosen as the creation point of the Yukon at various times for various—usually personal or political—reasons. It wasn't until 1949 that the Yukon officially traveled as far upstream as Whitehorse. The channel that flows by what is now the Territorial capital was called the Lewes River until then, and a cynic would say it was a purely political choice to call the river *Yukon* so the capital could sit on the water that defines its Territory.

Strictly applying the length and remoteness criteria, what is now called the Teslin River should be called the Yukon instead. More water flows through its channel than through the upper Yukon valley, and the Teslin is much longer, too.

Most through-paddlers and this book ignore these intricate arguments and travel from Whitehorse, Yukon Territory to the village of Emmonak, Alaska, several miles inland from the Bering Sea. This route works well not because these communities are necessarily strict geographic start and stop points of the Yukon, but because they are practical places to begin and end the journey. Whitehorse is the largest city in the Yukon Territory and the outlet of Marsh Lake just above town is the first body of water named *Yukon* on government maps. Whitehorse has regularly scheduled air service from all over the world, as well as an excellent infrastructure of canoe, outdoor, and grocery stores that make supplying the beginning of the trip quick, cheap, and convenient. Emmonak is the largest village on the delta and is a practical point to end the journey. Cargo and passenger planes use its gravel airstrip as a regional hub. Cargo prices from Emmonak to Anchorage are low because it is a dead-head haul for the empty planes after they've dropped their goods off in the villages. There is daily passenger service from Emmonak to Anchorage as well.

Alternate routes fulfill different requirements. The glacial lakes forming the headwaters above Whitehorse are some of the most spectacular bodies of water anywhere. They are wonderful to explore in a year with an unusually early spring when lake ice is melted and the river is flowing, leaving plenty of time to reach the Bering Sea around the beginning of August. Some people choose to hike over Chilkoot Pass, then paddle the lakes down to Dawson to recreate the gold rush journey of 1898. If Lake Laberge is late breaking up, floating the Teslin River until it joins the Yukon below the lake is an excellent route around the ice. Paddlers can also put in at Carmacks, roughly one hundred miles downriver from Whitehorse, to avoid a frozen Laberge. Although an expensive alternative, planes do fly from Whitehorse to drop paddlers off at the outlet of Lake Laberge.

The options for takeouts besides Emmonak are more limited. St. Marys has excellent air service. It sits about 70 miles upriver from the delta, and by leaving from there, you avoid the terrible weather, tides, and waves along the exposed mouth. Any other village along the river has air service, just not necessarily by planes large enough to handle a boat (a list of villages and plane service is detailed later). Villagers have been known to buy boats from drifters, but don't count on it, and don't expect more than a token payment if you do manage to sell the boat. Some fast paddlers travel along the Bering Sea coast to villages farther from the mouth, such as Nome to the north or even Dillingham to the south. Do not make this journey in an open canoe if you are still interested in life. Even in a sea kayak it is a challenge. There is very little shelter from the vicious storms along the coast and, even if you don't mind storms, the ice can move in very quickly in the fall. You would probably be so concerned with speed to beat the ice it would override your savoring many portions of the journey leading to the sea.

Paddling Skills

The two short rapids on the Yukon below Whitehorse require just intermediate paddling ability—provided you pay attention and run them properly. Steamship operators dynamited the channels nearly a hundred years ago and there is literally enough room to run a barge between the rocks.

Although these rapids are relatively easy, almost every inch of the Yukon can kill you. The silt load is incredible. The constant rasping of suspended sand against the boat hull will become a permanent background noise. Many people have drowned after capsizing when their pockets and boots filled with dirt and dragged them under. Above Fort Yukon, the river is particularly swift, sometimes traveling at well over 10 miles per hour, creating swirling eddies and undertows that can quickly drag you down. The water is breathtakingly cold, and can immobilize you or cause hypothermia if you manage to swim to shore but cannot quickly dry off and warm up. And any flat-water section, particularly the headwater lakes and the treeless delta, can quickly be blown into tremendous waves by storms. So, the water puts a premium not on technical whitewater-paddling skills, but on wariness and common sense. Travel close to the banks, never more than a quick hustle to shore in case the weather turns ugly. Carry extra food and have the patience and paperback books to camp and wait out bad weather, for days at a time if necessary. And always wear a lifejacket.

Timing

The trip will be fastest if you begin paddling as soon as the ice clears from the channel, usually by the last week of May or the first week of June. An early start allows you to catch the spring meltwater just as it begins to rise, then ride the swelling water as long as possible downriver. Plus, June is a relatively dry month and the weather is delightful. Most paddlers will want to reach the delta by early to middle August before the severe fall storms roll off the Bering Sea with increasing frequency and intensity.

These constraints make a relatively tight 8 to 11 week window to paddle 1,800 miles (2898 km). An early departure lets you do the trip more at your own pace, rather than a slog to the finish. The Yukon flows swiftly for the first half of the journey, and if you paddle steadily, it is possible to arrive at the delta without too much strain. But you must maintain traveling discipline and spend time on the water without getting bogged down in a town.

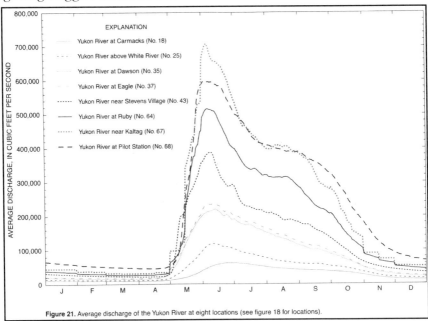

Figure 21. Average discharge of the Yukon River at eight locations (see figure 18 for locations).

Avg. Discharge Chart: Reproduced with permission from Brabets, Timothy P. and others, Environmental and Hydrologic Overview of the Yukon River Basin, Alaska and Canada. Water Resources Investigations Report 99-4202, US Geological Survey, Anchorage, AK, 2000.

Boat Type

The most popular type of paddling craft to complete the entire Yukon is a sea kayak, since it handles wind and waves well. Canoes are the most popular paddled boats on the relatively narrow channel between Whitehorse and Circle, but are a distant second choice as the rivers slows, widens, and approaches the ocean. Choose whichever boat type you are most comfortable and familiar with. Rafts of all flavors are strongly discouraged since they handle poorly in wind and are difficult to maneuver in narrow eddies.

Weather and Water

Ice tends to melt on the flowing river by the end of May, although ice berms can linger along the high-water mark well into June. If you wait to let the ice clear, it shouldn't cause too much difficulty. But there are exceptions.

It is easy to get fooled into thinking the ice has worked itself out of the channel. The Yukon flows north, so the headwaters melt first. The downriver ice dams the newly flowing water from the south and, depending on the year, can cause serious floods.

Ice blocks the northern end of Lake Laberge in this June view from Richtofen Island. The lake remains frozen well after the river begins flowing.

Lake Laberge stays frozen well past breakup on the flowing river. As the lake ice breaks up, it tends to clump into masses of cubes that are blown around by the wind. You can paddle onto the lake from Whitehorse, travel halfway across it, and encounter ice, which blocks your path. It is best to wait until the lake is completely clear of ice before crossing. However, if you do find ice on the lake, stick to the eastern shore—the right side headed down river—since the ice tends to mass up along the jagged left shore and the islands on that side.

Boat retailers in Whitehorse are an excellent source of information about current ice conditions.

The air is surprisingly warm when it's dry and sunny. This is usually delightful except that, the hotter it gets, the more likely it is a thunderstorm will erupt. The water is so cold through the upper river that when warm air hits the Yukon, the river manufactures its own weather. On warm days, clouds start forming above the channel in the morning, growing bigger and darker through the day, and finally explode into violent windstorms with lots of thunder and lightning and a smattering of cold rain by late afternoon. It is very difficult to control a boat in the hour or two these storms typically last, so it is best to get off the river and wait them out. If one develops on Lake Laberge, or on any of the upper headwater lakes, huge waves easily capable of swamping a boat can develop, so the prudent paddler is off the lakes well before the storm hits. When the weather turns hot, the best strategy is to wake up and begin paddling very early in the day, so you can have a full day's paddle done by the time the storm hits in the afternoon and it's time to pull off.

Thunderstorms frequently start forest fires in the early summer when it's still dry. There will likely be lots of smoke to see and smell. But, as long as you stick to the islands and gravel bars of the river, you should be safe.

As the Yukon approaches the Bering Sea, the air steadily cools and becomes more humid. Roughly after Galena or Koyukuk, expect consistent drizzle and a headwind. If it isn't wet and cold through here, you're just lucky. Storms are less frequent, but are more severe and long lasting.

Drinking Water

There is no real industrial pollution and very little giardia on the Yukon, but all water should be treated somehow before drinking, just to be safe. The exception to this is between Whitehorse and Lake Laberge, where even treated Yukon water shouldn't be drunk. The Whitehorse sewage treatment plant discharges effluent into the river, and it doesn't thoroughly settle out until about a third of the way across the still lake. This is a relatively short stretch of river, and loading up on water in Whitehorse should be more than sufficient to get the paddler through this section. If not, there are numerous tributaries to the main stem that have good water.

The Yukon is so silty that water filters plug up after only one or two uses below Houtalinqua, roughly 100 miles into the trip. Drinking water below this point either has to be boiled, then allowed to sit overnight, acquired from a clear tributary, or gathered from a town pump.

Gear

The major material obstacle to paddling the Yukon is getting a boat to the headwaters and pulling out of the delta. Through-paddlers will probably find it cheapest to buy a boat in Whitehorse and either sell it for a pittance on the delta or fly it back to Anchorage or Fairbanks. Rental boats along with return transportation are available in Whitehorse or Eagle if you are doing a segment of the upper river.

All other gear and equipment concerns are thoroughly discussed in the general paddling introduction.

International Concerns

Passports are now required for travel between the United States and Canada. What a wonderful world it once was, when all you needed was a driver's license and a smile to cross the border.

Almost all retailers in Whitehorse, Carmacks, and Dawson accept American dollars at an exchange rate that varies from store to store. Banks in Whitehorse and Dawson will give you a slightly more favorable rate than a retailer. Canadian dollars are not accepted by American businesses, so do not expect to use loonies farther downriver than Dawson. Visa is the universally accepted credit card in Canada. Discover Card, Master Card, and American Express are hardly ever accepted anywhere in the Yukon Territory and are accepted only by airlines in Alaska villages. In Canada, you can either charge phone calls with a Visa card or by calling a toll-free number to access your home long-distance service.

If you are traveling from the United States, remember that handguns are illegal in Canada. If you have a shotgun for bears, you will be required to purchase an annual gun permit for C$50 before entering Canada.

Maps

You have to patch together your own detailed maps. Mike Rourke has written an excellent guidebook, *Yukon River, Marsh Lake, Yukon to Circle, Alaska*, that covers the first 700 miles of the Yukon. This book is a labor of love and cannot be praised enough. The maps are detailed as well as meticulously accurate. The historical tidbits are well researched and illuminate the passing countryside so well the guide expands the canoeing experience. The only problem with this book is getting your hands on it. It is a photocopied, spiral-bound volume with limited distribution.

Gus Karpes has written two guides to the upper Yukon River. *Yukon River No.1* covers Whitehorse to Carmacks, and *Yukon River No. 2* describes Carmacks to Dawson. These books are more widely available than Rourke's and are published in a German-language edition, too.

Both of these guidebooks are available at Macs Fireweed Books in Whitehorse, YT, or through their website www.yukonbooks.com.

The individual section descriptions in this book detail the government map names needed for each river segment, but, if you are planning on doing the whole thing, all the maps needed are laid out in this table for convenience.

Guide Book	Guide Book	NRCanada 1:250,000	USGS 1:250,000
Rourke, Yukon, Marsh Lake to Circle	Karpes, The Yukon River No.1	Whitehorse	
✓	✓	Lake Laberge	
✓	✓	Glenlyon	
✓	Karpes, The Yukon River No. 2	Carmacks	
✓	✓	Stevenson Ridge	
✓	✓	Stewart River	
✓	✓	Dawson	
✓		Partie de 11	
✓			Eagle
✓			Circle
			Fort Yukon
			Beaver
			Livengood
			Tanana
			Melozitna
			Ruby
			Nulato
			Ophir
			Unalakeet
			Holy Cross
			Russian Mission
			Marshall
			Kwiguk

Rest and Resupply Points

All the villages on the following list have at least a small grocery store, public phone, washeteria, passenger air service, and a post office. These places are usually open for very limited hours during the week. An explanation of the unusual services offered by some towns and villages is in order:

Cargo: Served by cargo planes or buses big enough to handle a hard-shell canoe or kayak.

Grocery Store: Grocery store large enough to stock up several

River Mile/km	Town & Zip Code	Road	Cargo Plane	Grocery Store	Café
29/46.7	Whitehorse, YT,Y1A4N2	✓	✓	✓	✓
217/349.4	Carmacks, YT,Y0B1C0	✓		✓	✓
468/753.6	Dawson, YT,Y0B1G0	✓	✓	✓	✓
572/921.1	Eagle, AK 99738	✓			✓
723/1164.3	Circle, AK 99733	✓			✓
795/1280.2	Fort Yukon, AK 99740		✓	✓	✓
868/1397.7	Beaver, AK 99724				
955/1537.8	Stevens Village, AK 99774				
980/1578.1	Yukon Crossing	✓			✓
1035/1666.7	Rampart, AK 99767				
1103/1776.2	Tanana, AK 99777				✓
1223/1969.4	Ruby, AK 99768				
1273/2049.9	Galena, AK 99741		✓	✓	✓
1305/2101.4	Koyukuk, AK 99754				
1323/2130.4	Nulato, AK 99765				
1357/2185.2	Kaltag, AK 99748				
1468/2363.9	Grayling, AK 99590				
1487/2394.5	Anvik, AK 99558				
1526/2457.3	Holy Cross, AK 99602				
1596/2570.0	Russian Mission, AK 99657				
1640/2640.9	Marshall, AK 99585				
1689/2719.8	Pilot Station, AK 99650				
1710/2753.6	Pitkas Point, •AK 99658	•(use St. Marys PO)			
1710/2753.6	St. Marys, AK 99658		✓	✓	✓
1726/2779.4	Mt Village, AK 99632			✓	
1793/2887.3	Emmonak, AK 99581		✓	✓	✓

week's food and with reliable fresh fruit and vegetables, the gold standard for a fancy place.

Road: Access to a road. Whitehorse is the only city on a paved road; the rest are on gravel roads.

Café: Hope you like hamburgers and french fries, because that is what they have.

Yukon Crossing is not a village, just the junction of the Yukon River, the trans-Alaska pipeline, and the Dalton Highway. There is a truck stop here with motel, café, public telephone (time limited to ten minutes), and bus service to Fairbanks which hauls boats.

The village of St. Marys is also called Andreafsky on the map. It is not actually on the Yukon, but several miles up the Andreafsky River. St. Marys can be accessed by parking at Pitkas Point and walking the roughly 3 mile road between the two communities.

Below Koyukuk village there is a bar and liquor store locally called *Last Chance*. All the villages downriver from this point are dry, meaning that alcohol is illegal. Beaver and Stevens Village, upriver in the Yukon Flats, are dry, too.

Yukon River Guide

Whitehorse to Dawson

Miles: Whitehorse to Dawson: 468 miles (753.6 km)

Estimated Time: 10 to 14 days of steady paddling. A month would be more appropriate to stop and savor just a small selection of the interesting things to do along the way. Come to think of it, an entire summer wouldn't be enough time to thoroughly explore every deserving feature.

Water Class: I-II, plus one very short section of class III water at Five Finger Rapids.

Access: There is scheduled airline service—both passenger and cargo—to Whitehorse and Dawson, and private van service for the return trip from Carmacks or Dawson back to Whitehorse. The Alaska Highway passes through Whitehorse, the Klondike Highway through Carmacks, and the Klondike and Top of the World Highways pass through Dawson.

The Parks Highway Express runs a bus between Dawson and Fairbanks (1-888-600-6001).

Alaska Direct Buslines runs a weekly van between White-horse, Dawson, and Tok (1-800-770-6652).

In addition, private shuttles can be arranged through outfitters in Whitehorse for transportation—including boats and gear—at any place along the Yukon drainage accessible by road.

Planes:
Air North
Passenger Reservations and/or cargo:
USA (800) 764-0407   Canada (800) 661-0407
www.flyairnorth.com

Maps: The Natural Resources Canada 1:250,000 scale maps are:
Whitehorse
Lake Laberge
Glenlyon
Carmacks
Stevenson Ridge
Stewart River
Dawson

Guidebooks: Mike Rourke's guidebook *Yukon River, Marsh Lake, Yukon to Circle, Alaska*. Gus Karpes, *The Yukon River No.1*, covers the Whitehorse-to-Carmacks leg, and *The Yukon River No. 2*, details the river from Carmacks to Dawson.

Outfitters: Kanoe People has a good selection of canoes and kayaks for sale and/or rent, as well as the full complement of additional paddling gear, including life vests, paddles, and maps. They also rent boats for shorter trips and arrange transportation to and from Whitehorse with either your boat or theirs.

Kanoe People
Whitehorse, YT
(867) 668-4899
info@kanoepeople.com
www.kanoepeople.com

Eagle Canoe also rents canoes and arranges transportation for the sections between Whitehorse, Dawson, and Circle.

Eagle Canoe Rentals
PO Box 4
Eagle City, AK 99738
(907) 547-2203
paddleak@aptalaska.net

An excellent local source of maps and guides is:

Mac's Fireweed Books
203 Main Street
Whitehorse, YT Y1A 2B2
(867) 668-6104 or 1-800-661-0508
macsbooks@yukonbooks.com
http://yukonbooks.com

The Whitehorse Chamber of Commerce can be a good source to learn about services in town. They maintain a list of members on the Internet at www.yukonweb.com.

The *Milepost*, available through www.themilepost.com, is a thick, advertisement-crammed book published annually. It details northern highways, and can also be an excellent source of information on services in Whitehorse or anyplace in the Yukon or Alaska accessible by road.

Rest and Restocking Facilities: The three metropolitan areas in this section are Whitehorse, Carmacks, and Dawson.

With roughly 35,000 people, Whitehorse is the largest city in the Yukon Territory and has all the amenities of a medium-sized town: groceries, banks (including currency exchange), and many motels and campgrounds. There are several outdoor gear stores, including some that sell canoes and kayaks. If you have more time than money, you can usually buy a boat from the classified ads in the paper. Boat prices in Whitehorse will probably be slightly higher than in the southern provinces because of higher shipping costs, but buying in Whitehorse can be substantially cheaper than bringing in your own boat.

Because of size, weight, and material restrictions on airplane luggage, it is easiest to stock up on many items in Whitehorse rather than bring them with you. Fuel, pepper spray for bears, and fresh groceries are readily available with an excellent selection from a choice of grocery stores. Paddles, lifejackets, and other bulky items are also available in town.

Carmacks is much smaller than Whitehorse, but has restaurants, a small but well-stocked grocery store, phones, motels, and a RCMP post. There is a municipal campground on the river just past the Klondike Highway bridge, although staying on a gravel bar above town is a more peaceful option.

Dawson, the second largest town in the Yukon, is a tourist town with a groove. There are plenty of hotels and restaurants, a hostel, campgrounds with showers, and laundromats. The two grocery stores in Dawson are better stocked than those in any other town downriver except for Galena or St. Marys. It is an excellent opportunity for through-paddlers to stock the food bag.

Weather: June and early July have mostly dry, sunny, continental weather. August tends to be wetter and colder.

Section Discussion

Whitehorse to Dawson is the most popular stretch of the Yukon River to paddle for very good reason. The country is sublime. The water swiftly flows past ghost towns, wrecked steamships, and gold dredges. Campsites are firm and close to the water. The bugs aren't too bad if you camp on gravel bars. The weather—unless it's raining—can be sunny and warm. The nearly perfect conditions attract paddlers from all over the world. This part of the Yukon is a Canadian Heritage River, an official designation which, as a practical matter, means campsites are well developed around the many historical towns along the bank, including gazebos, outhouses, and interpretive signs in four languages.

As you might guess from the roughly 12 day travel time to cover the nearly 500 miles (805.2 km) in this section, the Yukon flies through here. The speed makes the paddling very easy—the biggest physical effort is to jam your paddle in the water to keep the bow from getting knocked off course by boiling eddies. It is an excellent way to gradually get into shape at the beginning of the trip. But there are disadvantages to the fast water. If something cool pops up unexpectedly—say, an abandoned cabin on shore—you don't have time to cross the river to see it before your boat is washed downriver. Frequently, the only way to check something out is by looking over your shoulder as it fades from view. To sightsee properly, you have to line up on the spot well before getting there. The back eddy along the bank is quite narrow and the boat must be completely in it to park—the double pontoons of a cataraft are particularly awkward to land. And, last, the speeding current creates lots of boils, swirls, and unexpected eddies that make the river extremely dangerous for swimming. Don't flip the boat.

During June, the water level can rise very quickly, surging over a foot overnight at times when it gets hot. Be sure to camp high each night the water is rising.

And, be sure to flip over and tie down your boat at night. Wind can pick up unexpectedly and blow it away.

Whitehorse to Carmacks

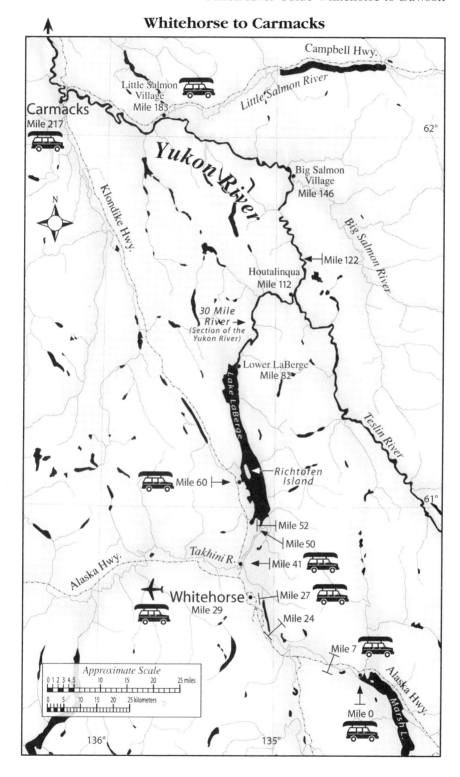

Campbell Hwy.

Little Salmon Village
Mile 183

Little Salmon River

Carmacks
Mile 217

62°

Yukon River

Big Salmon Village
Mile 146

Big Salmon River

Klondike Hwy.

N

Mile 122

Houtalinqua
Mile 112

30 Mile River →
(Section of the Yukon River)

Teslin River

Lower LaBerge
Mile 82

Lake LaBerge

61°

← Richtofen Island

Mile 60

Mile 52

Mile 50

Takhini R.

Mile 41

Alaska Hwy.

Mile 27

Whitehorse
Mile 29

Mile 24

Mile 7

Alaska Hwy.

Approximate Scale

0 1 2 3 4 5   10   15   20   25 miles

0   5   10   15   20   25 kilometers

Mile 0

Marsh L.

136°   135°

47

Carmacks to Coffee Creek

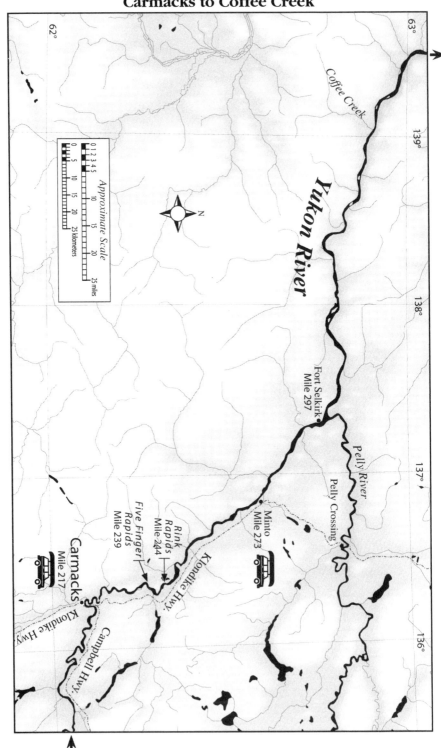

Coffee Creek to Dawson

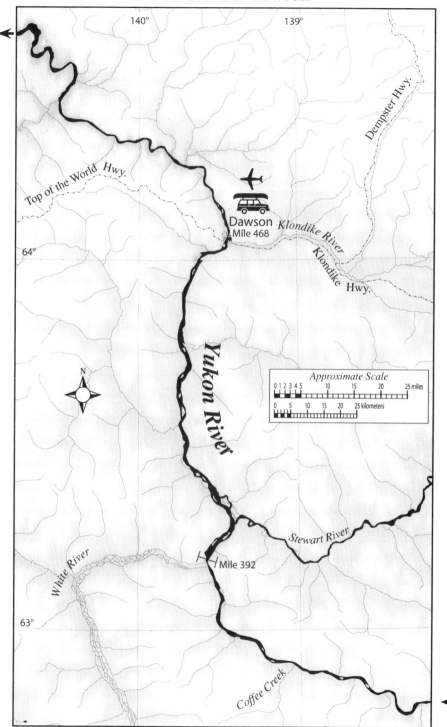

140°   139°

Dempster Hwy.

Top of the World Hwy.

Dawson
Mile 468

Klondike River

Klondike Hwy.

64°

Yukon River

N

Approximate Scale

0 1 2 3 4 5   10   15   20   25 miles

0   5   10   15   20   25 kilometers

Stewart River

Mile 392

White River

63°

Coffee Creek

Significant Points

Mile 0 (0 km): There is a small public campground near the outlet of Marsh Lake. The lake has a number of second homes along the shore. Don't worry, the Yukon quickly becomes much more remote. If camping between here and Whitehorse, look along the right bank, the side opposite from the Alaska Highway.

Mile 7 (11.3 km): Stick to the right and go around the small control dam through a series of locks with well-illustrated instructions. A boat launch sits on the right bank, by the Alaska Highway bridge.

Mile 24 (38.6 km): Miles Canyon. This canyon swamped and drowned many gold rush boaters, but is now drowned itself by the Whitehorse Hydroelectric Dam. No longer a canyon, it is now Lake Schwatka.

Mile 27 (43.2 km): Portage around the dam by sticking to the right side and following the road that parallels the fish ladder. Put in just below the powerhouse and watch for the current at the base of the tailrace. This is the last dam on the Yukon or any other river in this book.

This pre-dam view of Miles Canyon shows the obstacle gold rush prospectors had to pass. Modern paddlers will find the water considerably easier to navigate, but less exciting.
(Alaska State Library, P.E. Larss Collection)

Mile 29 (46.7 km): The Yukon is a wide, fast creek through Whitehorse with many gravel bars, riffles, and informal public access points. Then, for about 20 river miles, it curves its muddy way around islands and through bends, past farms, vacation homes, and occasionally within sight of the Alaska and Klondike highways.

Mile 41 (66 km): The downstream point at the Takhini River mouth is an access to the Klondike Highway.

Mile 50 (80 km): If it is at all windy, you will want to camp on the protected river and wait until the weather calms before paddling Lake Laberge. The last good camp is on the bend here, with an outhouse and cleared tenting spots.

Mile 52 (83.7 km): Passing through a set of pilings that used to direct the current of the river, the Yukon enters Lake Laberge, location for the Robert Service poem, *The Cremation of Sam McGee*. Thirty-one miles long, Laberge is one of the most beautiful bodies of water in the world. It's muddy when the river first flows in, but the water soon becomes as clear and green as a gem. The wind usually blows from south to north, so, although it's a still body of water, under the right conditions, it can be a fast paddle. The emphasis is on the phrase, *right conditions*. Lake Laberge is also one of the most dangerous stretches of the whole Yukon.

The water is frigid. When warm air hits the cold lake, it makes very nasty thunderstorms that quickly blow up from a seemingly clear sky. Stick close to shore, and if black clouds start bunching up, hustle to shelter. The right shore is a little straighter than the left, so it's a faster paddle, but there aren't quite as many camp spots as on the left side.

Ice can also be a problem on Laberge if you are starting early in the year, like in June. It is one of the last spots to break up on the river. The ice tends to bunch up on the northern and western sides of the lake. If you paddle halfway across the lake and a line of ice chunks blocks the way, you might have to do some camping. This is one of the reasons some of the best safety equipment is an overstuffed food bag and a small library of paperback books. If the ice is broken into chunks, the wind can move it around in a matter of days, clearing the lake for travel.

Mile 60 (96.6 km): The Lake Laberge campground sits on the left shore, just before the southernmost point of Richtofen Island. There is access to the Klondike Highway as well as sixteen fee camping spots.

The hull of the steamship Casca I marks the shore of Lower Laberge. There are interpretive signs, firepits, and an outhouse for visitors to this old steamer and telegraph station.

Mile 82 (132.0 km): The abandoned steamer station Lower Laberge marks the end of the lake and the beginning of the 30 Mile River, the stretch below Lake Laberge to the Teslin River. This is the only clear stretch of flowing water on the Yukon, and the water is gorgeous. It twists its way through high, silt-walled canyons and fast riffles. There is mind-boggling good fishing, where you can actually fish the main channel with a fishing rod. The water flows so quickly it is a short day's paddle, but if you took three days to cover these 30 miles, you could still feel that you hadn't spent enough time here.

Mile 112 (180.4 km): Houtalinqua is an abandoned telegraph station and steamer maintenance camp. There are a number of old cabins with interpretive signs. The campsites are very well developed, with a gazebo, firepits, and outhouse. The area can be quite popular with boaters. The highlight is the steamer *Evelyn* on Shipyard Island just downstream from Houtalinqua. The boat is in good shape and the maintenance building, while leaning to the side, is one of the best preserved buildings on the river.

Below the Teslin River mouth and the abandoned village of Houtalinqua, the river turns muddy again. The silt will last until the Bering Sea and water filters will no longer work reliably. (For an in-depth discussion on managing drinking water, please see the Long-Distance Paddling section at the beginning of this book).

The canyons open up from here and the water flows a little faster and more smoothly since there are no longer as many shallow riffles.

Mile 122 (196.6 km): At lower water, the hull of the wrecked steamship *SS Klondike* is visible, stranded on a sandbar in the middle of the channel.

Mile 146 (235.1 km): Big Salmon Village is an abandoned native village at the mouth of Big Salmon River. This is quite a popular spot with boaters. There are a number of restored cabins and standard camping facilities.

Mile 183 (294.6 km): Little Salmon Village is also an abandoned native village. There are a number of graves just past the mouth of the Little Salmon River. The gravel Campbell Highway is nearby and there is a spur off it leading to the river. The highway will intermittently appear on the east bluffs until Carmacks.

Mile 217 (349.4 km): The town of Carmacks is clearly foreshadowed by the appearance of the Klondike Highway bridge. There is a municipal campground just past the bridge on the left bank and C$10 will pay for a spot. However, since it is right next to the road, most people will find a camping spot on a gravel bar on the river more attractive. Paddlers just stopping off for a few hours usually go past the campground landing and beach on the left bank in front of the RCMP post, where there is a public telephone. In addition, Carmacks is a well-stocked town from a paddler's point of view, with restaurants, grocery store, and laundromat, all on the left bank and within a quick walk. Downstream, the Klondike Highway will appear and disappear along the right bank until Minto.

Mile 239 (384.9 km): The next major obstacle is Five Finger Rapids. Five basalt towers reach up through the river, and create one of the few rocky rapids on the Yukon. The gap on the far right of the river has the smoothest passage. Although the water can reach Class III with a few standing waves at the outlet of the rapids, the channel was repeatedly blasted with dynamite to clear the rocks enough to let a steamship pass.

Every few years, though, it seems that some paddlers drown in these rapids. This is nearly always due to a lack of attention and going through one of the passages toward the left while not worrying enough about keeping the boat straight through the rough water. As long as you concentrate, pass through the far right gap, and treat the obstacle with respect, there should be no problems in a human-powered boat.

Mile 244 (390.4 km): Rink Rapids is a Class II collection of shallow water flowing over rocks. It's so shallow it doesn't quite qualify as rapids, since it's almost impossible to paddle through. Follow the broad, smoothly flowing channel along the right bank to avoid it with room to spare. Look for the wreck of the steamship *Casca* II on the left bank of the island, just below the rocks.

Mile 273 (439.5 km): Minto has a few scattered residents and two campgrounds, one government owned, the other private with showers, laundry, and convenience store. There is access to the Klondike Highway.

Mile 297 (478.3 km): Fort Selkirk stretches along the left bank of the Yukon just below the mouth of the Pelly River. Restored through the cooperative efforts of the Yukon government and the Selkirk First Nation, this abandoned town is a highlight of the trip. Log buildings date from the late 1800s to the early 1950s, at which point the town was abandoned in favor of a location next to the newly built Klondike Highway. A caretaker is stationed here throughout the summer to answer questions. There is a small campground as well.

The restored town of Ft. Selkirk, one of the first settlements in the territory, is a highlight of the upper Yukon. There is a visitor's center and full time interpretive guide who grew up there. The town is only accessible by boat.

Mile 392 (631.2 km): The White River brings in so much silt and water to the Yukon that the channel changes significantly below the mouth. It's called the White River because it carries so much glacial silt it's milky. The grit makes innumerable sandbars and snag mounds, and the water moves even faster. The channel almost doubles in size and can be windy and choppy due to the large fetch. There are numerous gravel bars and islands with excellent, frequent camps all the way to Dawson. The current is particularly swift.

Mile 468 (753.6 km): The town of Dawson marks the end of this section of the Yukon. The water flows very swiftly through the canyon, so stick to the left bank well before the ferry landing. At the landing, it is a short portage up a path through the trees to a small, primitive campground run by the local tribe. Or, from the landing, you can also take the path through the trees and turn left to follow the gravel road a short way to an international hostel. Both the hostel and the campground have showers. Also on the left bank, but just a little downriver past the ferry landing, a long, smooth beach sits in front of the Yukon Territory's government campground. If you park your boat at the top of the beach, you can wander through the woods paralleling the river to find an empty camp spot. The advantages of staying here are the short portage and not having to park right by the ferry landing in front of the vehicles lined up to take the ferry across to Dawson. The disadvantage is that the government campground does not have showers.

Dawson, the second-largest town in the Yukon Territory, is a fully stocked tourist destination across the river from the campgrounds. There are no easy places to stay with a boat in town. There are two grocery stores downtown, a number of campgrounds catering to RVs, a hostel, laundromats, and numerous hotels. A free ferry crosses the Yukon 24 hours a day, so you can camp at one of the campgrounds on the left bank and spend the day in town on the right bank. Legalized gambling starts at night, and don't forget to have a Sourtoe Cocktail—a shot of liqueur with an embalmed toe at the bottom of the glass that has to touch your lips. Try not to actually swallow the

The author achieves membership in the Sourtoe Cocktail Club.

Yukon River Guide

Dawson to Circle

Distance: 255 miles (410.6 km)

Estimated Time: 5 to 7 days

Water Class: I-II. The current is extremely swift with many boiling eddies through this stretch. The water is roughest along the cliff bases, so if you hang back a little from the rock walls the going is smoother. When the wind blows over the wide channel through here, even flat water can quickly be whipped into whitecaps.

Access: Dawson has excellent road and air service. See the previous section for detailed information.

Forty-Mile is a ghost town with two very friendly caretakers at the end of a gravel spur road off Yukon Highway 9. There are many delightful places to camp under the shelter of old roofs, but there are no services here.

Eagle sits at the terminus of the gravel Taylor highway. There is also chartered and scheduled air service in small planes.

Circle sits at the terminus of the gravel Steese highway. There is also charter and small plane service.

Maps: Gus Karpes' guidebook ***Yukon River, Marsh Lake, Yukon to Circle, Alaska*** provides excellent history as well as detailed, accurate river maps.

The Canadian 1:250,000 maps are:
Dawson
Partie de 11

The United States Geological Survey 1:250,000 maps are:
Eagle
Circle

Outfitters: Eagle Canoe rents canoes for the shorter sections of the Yukon-between Whitehorse, Dawson, and Circle.
Eagle Canoe Rentals
PO Box 4
Eagle City, AK 99738
(907) 547-2203
paddleak@aptalaska.net

Yukon Charley National Preserve contact information:
National Park Service
PO Box 167
Eagle, AK 99738
(907) 547-2233

Rest and Restocking: Eagle has a small grocery store, campground, bed and breakfast, and restaurant. The U.S. Customs Service maintains a post here, and you will have to check in with them if arriving from Canada.

Circle, population 100, has a motel, small store, café, bed and breakfast, and post office all within easy walk of the beach.

Weather: The climate is roughly the same through here as the upper part of the river—semi-arid, with occasional short, violent thunderstorms. The days are noticeably longer than in Whitehorse.

Section Discussion

Leaving Dawson it feels like the Yukon falls off a cliff—if anything, the water flows even faster through here than through the Whitehorse-to-Dawson section. Five to seven days is a very conservative estimate for the travel time—if the water level is high, this stretch can take just four days if you push for time. The current flies.

The channel grows wider, especially after the addition of the Forty-Mile River, and the water can get much rougher when the wind picks up. Gusts you can paddle through on, say, the Thirty-Mile River, can force you to pull over to shore and wait for the weather to clear.

This section is notable for the heavy concentration of public use cabins through the Yukon-Charley National Preserve. These are nice places to stay to get out of the rain, but can be so buggy that gravel bars are more appealing camps. Bunk space in the cabins is first come, first served. The Park Service is in the midst of a building spree through this section of river and may well have added new visitor facilities since this guide was published. If cabin living is your thing, then check with the Park Service's office in Eagle.

Two cruise ships travel between Dawson and Eagle each day. These boats can be a severe hazard. They throw out a huge wake and do not always slow down and swing wide for paddlers. You will likely have to turn to face the oncoming wall of water to avoid getting sloshed sideways after they pass.

Dawson to Eagle

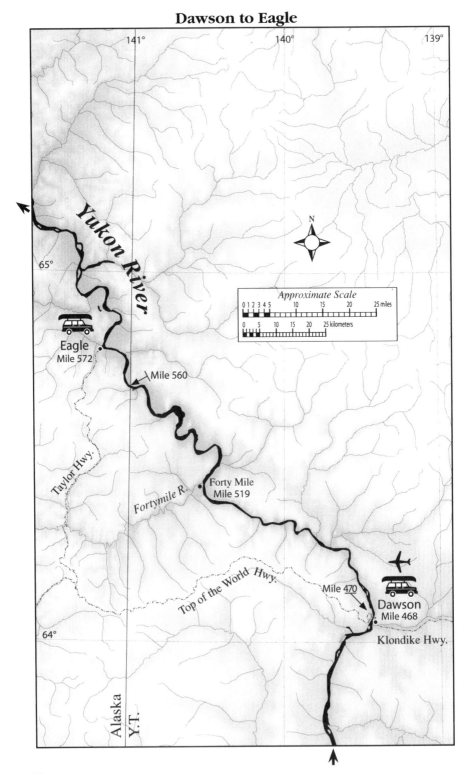

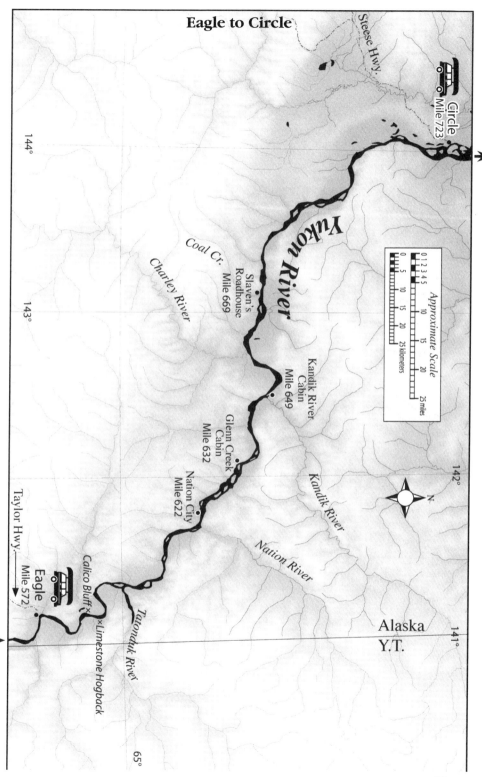

Eagle to Circle

Steese Hwy.

Circle
Mile 723

144°

Yukon River

Coal Cr.

Slaven's
Roadhouse
Mile 669

Charley River

143°

Kandik River
Cabin
Mile 649

Approximate Scale

0 1 2 3 4 5

0   5   10   15   20   25 kilometers

0   5   10   15   20   25 miles

Glenn Creek
Cabin
Mile 632

Nation City
Mile 622

142°

Kandik River

N

Taylor Hwy.

Eagle
Mile 572

Calico Bluff

×Limestone Hogback

Tatonduk River

Nation River

Alaska
Y.T.

141°

65°

Significant Points

Mile 470 (753.6 km): Follow the left bank as you leave Dawson and look for the steamship graveyard just below town.

Mile 519 (835.7 km): The abandoned mining town of Forty Mile sits

on the left bank, just above the mouth of the Fortymile River. This ghost town is full of rotting buildings, rusty machinery, and old cabins. Friendly caretakers watch over it. If you want company or just need a spot to dry out, the old stamp mill makes a fine shelter.

Mile 560 (901.8): A straight clearing through the trees marks the United States - Canada border.

A sign welcomes travelers to the ghost town of 40 Mile.

Mile 572 (921.1 km): The city of Eagle. Remember to check in with U.S. Customs here. In addition, the village of 150 year-round residents can be a nice break from the river or a put-in or takeout spot since it sits at the terminus of the partially paved Taylor Highway.

As you float down the river, Eagle Village is the first settlement along the left bank. There are no services here. Then the cruise ship docks unmissably appear. The customs agent frequently works from this spot and will sometimes hail you from here. This public landing is a short walk to downtown. To save yourself the stroll, float past here to the main city dock, which is at the base of the steel-covered bank—Eagle, like almost all Yukon River towns, is sited on a cutbank so steamships could dock in the deeper water.

Despite its small size, Eagle has many services for travelers. A bed and breakfast sits right on the bank, as well as a general store with showers, a café, and motel. The BLM campground costs $8 per night, but is outside of town, away from the river. Take a right on Fourth Avenue, then go past Fort Egbert. The post office is a few blocks in from the river and the route is marked with signs. There is also a museum and a number of restored buildings at Fort Egbert. The National Park Service maintains a visitor center at the end of the airstrip with books and maps for sale, as well as personnel to answer questions about the upcoming Yukon-Charley Preserve section.

Mile 622 (1001.6 km): Nation City sits on the left bank, just down-river from the mouth of the Nation River. Christopher "Phonograph" Nelson built the Nation Bluff cabin in 1935; the National Park Service restored it for public use in 1995. An old road leads into the woods for about seven miles, where it dead-ends at an old mining site, which is private property.

Mile 632 (1017.7 km): The Glenn Creek public cabin is plainly visible from the river. Originally a hunting camp built in the 1950s by Walter Le Fevre, an optometrist from Fairbanks, it is now a nice place for paddlers to get out of the rain.

Mile 649 (1038.4): The Kandik River Public Use Cabin is at the end of a .25 mile trail up the Kandik River from the Yukon. This log cabin with a sod roof was built in 1981 to support its builder's subsistence lifestyle.

Mile 669 (1077.3 km): Slaven's Roadhouse sits on the left bank just below the mouth of Coal Creek. The visitor center and public-use cabin here are run by the National Park Service and can be a very good stop to both sleep under a roof and get some human company. If your legs are withered from too much paddling, you can give them a nice stretch by walking a mile up the gravel road to gaze at the Coal Creek dredge, which mined gold from the creek gravel until the 1960s. It's a nice walk, assuming the mosquitoes aren't their usual swarming, vicious selves.

You can walk four miles up through those mosquitoes to Coal Creek Cabin, a public use cabin. This small, one room former miner's cabin was built in the 1930s and was restored in 1999. It is now part of a larger Park Service operations complex which includes an airstrip and other, non-public buildings.

Mile 723 (1164.3 km): Circle marks the end of the hills and the begin-ning of the Flats. The town of roughly 100 people sits at the terminus of the partially paved Steese Highway. The road access means it has many services despite its small size: small grocery store, café, post office, fuel, liquor store, and motel. A public-use campground sits on the beach. Circle is a fine place to rest and get some town time. Just a 160 mile drive to Fairbanks, it's also a great spot to begin or end a shorter trip on the Yukon.

Despite being the site of the first major gold rush in Alaska, Circle is much less touristy than Dawson. There will be a few RVs parked in the campground, but that's about it. It is named Circle because the founding miners originally though it sat directly on the Arctic Circle line, but actually it is a little over 50 miles due south of it. There is a small graveyard with headstones from the late 1800s, ancient markers by Alaska standards. Just follow the gravel road upriver from the landing to a barricade, and then follow the path through the trees and bugs for around 10 minutes to reach the graves.

Yukon River Guide

The Flats, or Circle to Yukon Crossing

Distance: 257 miles (413.8 km)

Estimated Time: 5 to 7 days

Water Class/Potential Hazards: Class I. Halfway Whirlpool, halfway between Circle and Fort Yukon, can spin boats around and keep them within its current for the better part of a day. To avoid this nasty piece of water, stick to the left shore.

Access: Alaska Airlines provides passenger and air cargo service from Fort Yukon to Fairbanks and Anchorage.
Alaska Airlines
www.alaskaair.com
(800) 252-7522
Alaska Airlines charges for cargo by weight and volume. If your boat does not collapse, it can be fairly expensive to fly it out, since there is a minimum weight charge. Call Alaska Airlines before you leave if you plan to put your boat and gear on a plane from Fort Yukon.
Frontier Flying Service has passenger service to Fort Yukon, too.
Frontier Flying Service
(800) 478-6779
www.frontierflying.com
There is daily bus service from Yukon Crossing to Fairbanks run by:
Dalton Highway Express
(907) 452-3553
www.daltonhighwayexpress.com
They take canoes, kayaks, and gear into Fairbanks for a reasonable additional fare. Just call them from the café when you get there, requesting a pickup. Sometimes there is an available seat in the van and you can be in Fairbanks that evening; sometimes it might be a day or two to wait for a van with a boat rack.

Maps: USGS 1:250,000 quads:
Circle
Fort Yukon
Beaver
Livengood

Rest and Restocking: For a description of Circle, see the previous section.

Fort Yukon, on the junction of the Porcupine and Yukon Rivers, is the first village on this trip not attached to a road. Home to roughly 600 people, it is quite large by Bush Alaska standards, and has a full range of services, including frequent large plane air service, bed and breakfasts, bank, and a decent-size grocery store.

Beaver and Stevens Village are the two other villages within the Yukon Flats. Both of these communities are quite small and only have limited services, such as a post office, telephone, small airstrip, and washeteria. Alcohol is illegal in these two villages.

Yukon Crossing, the local name for the spot where the Dalton Highway and the Trans-Alaska Pipeline cross the Yukon, is not actually a village, but there are services here: motel, café, fuel, and public phone, but no grocery store. The Bureau of Land Management maintains a small visitor information cabin staffed by friendly volunteer caretakers.

Weather: The Yukon Flats is a desert; it gets less than 10 inches of rain a year. Although it can get quite hot in the summer—Fort Yukon has the highest temperature recorded in Alaska, 101 degrees—it will mostly be between 50 and 80 degrees Fahrenheit from June to August. However, there can be frequent, violent thunderstorms in the afternoon and when it rains, it is cold. After all, you are right along the Arctic Circle.

Section Description

The river changes character dramatically when three islands split the channel just past Circle. Leaving the confining hills to the south, the Yukon now sprawls across the plain in a seemingly endless mess of islands, sloughs, and gravel bars. There are few landmarks to orient by, and it is difficult to determine a precise location. Even if you do know where you are—say, around Fort Yukon or if you have a GPS—the river channel changes every year as the water erodes and rearranges the soft sediment. The Fort Yukon USGS map, last updated in 1995, will be only a conceptual guide. So, rather than cutting through the inside bends and islands to shorten the journey like the first 700 miles, the best way to travel through the Flats is to let the boat drift a bit. If the wind is fairly light, your boat will naturally find the main channel, avoiding meandering sloughs. If it does seem like you are in a slough, don't worry, just keep paddling ahead. It is impossible to get lost through here—eventually the main channel will reappear. It just might take the better part of a day. A little patience goes a long way sometimes.

There is a substantial drop-off in paddler traffic beyond Circle. There won't be any more interpretive signs or formal camping areas. Fish wheels and fish camps dot the banks around Fort Yukon, and skiff traffic will pick up as well. This is the beginning of Bush Alaska.

The water maintains its fast pace all the way to Fort Yukon, where it begins to steadily slow until a bit before Joe Devlin Island. From here to roughly Kings Slough Island, the water is optimistically described as sluggish. From Kings Slough until the canyons just before Yukon Crossing, the water all but stops as it pools up behind the Fort Hamlin Hills. The distant Brooks Range and the southern White Mountains will pop up occasionally from the blue haze and tease you with their nearness. Don't believe you're out of the Flats until you pass Stevens Village.

It is useless to fight a headwind between Kings Slough and Stevens Village. The wind usually dies in the cooler evening, so you might want to rest during the day and paddle through the light night. The sudden transition from plains to canyon just past Stevens Village can create very strong, localized thunderstorms that can force a paddler to shore for several days to wait out the nasty weather. Once again, carry more than enough food.

Fort Yukon is the farthest north the Yukon River travels—there are 20 miles or so of river actually above the Arctic Circle, the southernmost point the sun doesn't set on the solstice. If you leave Whitehorse at the beginning of June, the timing works out well to arrive precisely on that day (around June 21, the actual day varies year to year).

Circle to Yukon Flats

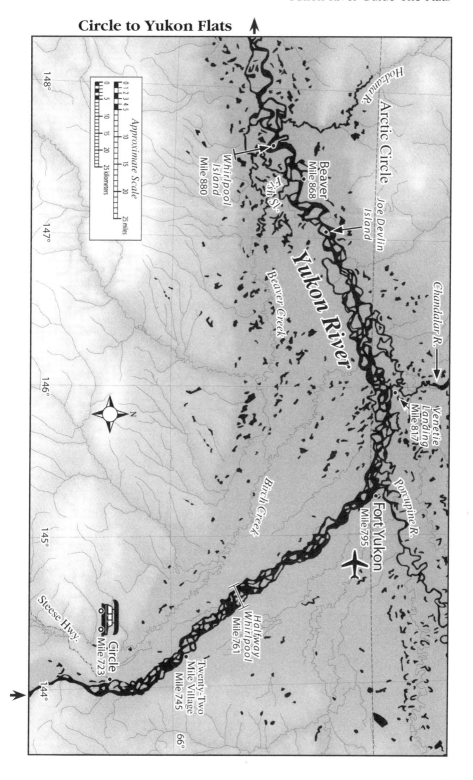

Yukon Flats to Yukon Crossing

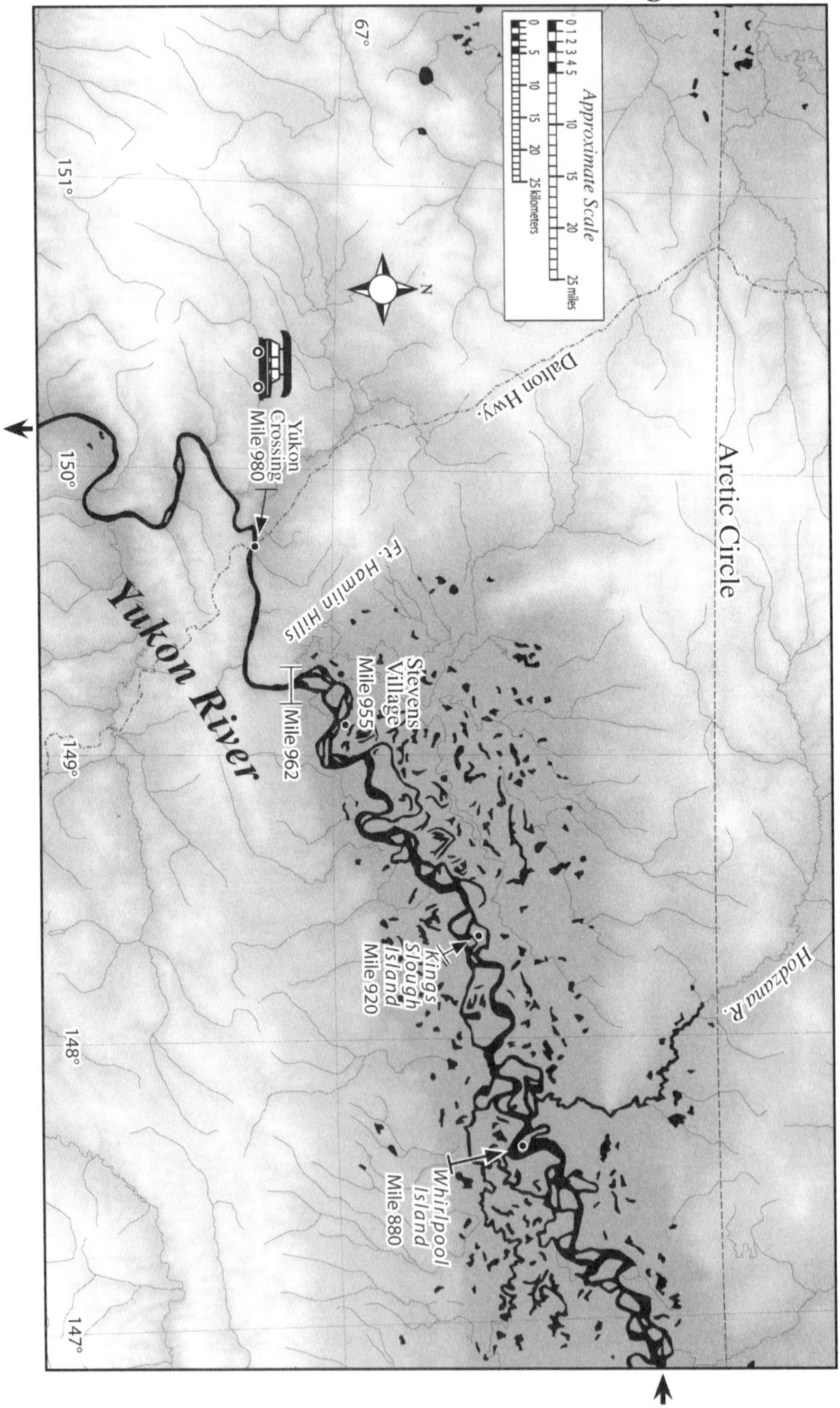

Approximate Scale

0 1 2 3 4 5

0 5 10 15 20 25 kilometers

0 5 10 15 20 25 miles

Yukon
Crossing
Mile 980

Dalton Hwy.

Arctic Circle

Yukon River

Ft. Hamlin Hills

Mile 962

Stevens
Village
Mile 955

Kings
Slough
Island
Mile 920

Hodzana R.

Whirlpool
Island
Mile 880

Significant Points

Mile 745 (1199.7 km): Twenty-Two Mile Village is a small collection of fish camps set back in the trees. You will probably see a few skiffs parked on the beach or maybe hear a chainsaw in the woods, but those are the only indications of this landmark discernible from the river. It is not a bad idea to time the 22 mile trip from Circle to here to determine the river pace. This way, you can navigate by your watch, and start sticking to the left bank 10 miles past here to avoid the Halfway Whirlpool.

Mile 761 (1225.4 km): Halfway Whirlpool. This current along the right bank can swirl your boat around for several hours before finally releasing it. Start sticking to the left bank well before you get here to avoid it. If you do get caught in it, don't panic. The water isn't rough, it just prevents forward progress. Calmly choose a moment when the current is slower and work yourself out.

Mile 795 (1280.2 km): Fort Yukon. The Yukon River is officially north of the Arctic Circle now. The airplanes flying overhead warn of the village long before you get there. Fort Yukon is a wet village (alcohol is legal), whose airport serves as a transportation hub to surrounding

This view of Joe Devlin Island shows how difficult it can be to navigate on the Yukon Flats. The main channel is to the left and a slough to the right. Although potentially handy at this spot, a GPS is only marginally useful in most other places in the Flats since the channels change from year to year-or even from season to season. It is more important to follow the strongest current rather than be at a precise point.

dry villages (alcohol is illegal). Many people come to Fort Yukon just to drink. Camping on the beach is not recommended and if you plan to spend the night you should either have friends in the village or stay at a bed and breakfast.

Fort Yukon is one of the oldest continuously occupied communities on the Yukon, founded as a fur-trading fort by the Hudson Bay Company in 1847. Being British, the HBC was forced out when the United States purchased the Alaska Territory in 1867, moving up the Porcupine River toward Canada. The site of a large missile warning station during the Cold War, Fort Yukon is now a largely Native village centered on a subsistence lifestyle.

Hudson Stuck, Archdeacon of the Yukon, first person to ascend Denali, founder of mission hospitals, and author of many of the best books on Alaska travel, is buried here.

The mouth of the Porcupine River, the Yukon's second-largest tributary, is just past town. There are many sloughs and islands where it sluggishly joins the river, and it is hard to tell it joins the flows at all.

Mile 817 (1307.2 km): A road leads roughly seven miles from Venetie Landing to the Chandalar River village of Venetie. I have paddled by here twice and have never seen the Landing. It is off in a side channel and you have to deliberately seek it to find it.

Mile 868 (1397.7 km): Beaver is a small village with 84 people and few services. To stop here, stick to the right bank well before the village and follow the slough to the beach. It is easy to miss the channel Beaver sits on and follow Fish Slough instead, so don't panic if you never see this landmark.

Mile 880 (1417.1 km): Whirlpool Island and Whirlpool Slough don't have active whirlpools associated with them.

Mile 920 (1481.5 km): The river all but stops flowing just past Kings Slough Island. Time to start working for the miles.

Mile 955 (1537.8 km): Stevens Village is a small community with minimal services. Stick to the right bank as you round the bend, and you can park on the beach.

Mile 962 (1549.1 km): Yeehaw! Back in the hills! But the current doesn't begin to pick up until the trans-Alaska pipeline is within sight, another 15 miles or so into the Fort Hamlin Hills. There are many fish camps through the canyon and lots of skiff traffic as well—people motor out from the public landing at the Dalton Highway crossing.

Mile 980 (1578.1 km): Yukon Crossing. There is no village here, but there is more activity than in many communities along the river.

Everyone worries about bears and moose, but marmots can be destructive, too. The bold rodents at Yukon Crossing chewed holes in a dry bag to get at the food, forcing a day off for repairs.

Land ownership here is complicated, unposted, and changes quickly. If camping here, float until just before the Dalton Highway bridge. There are some small flat spots on the river terraces with tent-size gaps in the willows that block the wind. Not many people walk through here and you will have a degree of privacy. As you float directly beneath the bridge, there are a number of beached skiffs owned by Alyeska Pipeline, the operator of the trans-Alaska pipeline. These are oil spill containment boats and are parked here in case of an emergency. The first boat ramp just past the abutment is gravel, owned by Stevens Village. It is open to villagers only. The concrete ramp just past it is the public landing and is open to everyone. There will almost certainly be several pickups and boat trailers parked here since it is a popular spot to put in. If you follow the road away from the bank, within a hundred yards will be a combination motel, café, and gas station. They have fee showers and a credit card only telephone, with calls limited to ten minutes. This is the last time a highway touches the Yukon River, and it can be a very good place to stop for a couple days or to end a shorter trip. There is bus service to Fairbanks.

Yukon River Guide

Yukon Crossing to Galena

Distance: 293 miles (471.7 km)

Estimated Time: 7 to 10 days

Water Class/Hazards: Class I-II. The Yukon River is almost entirely flat water from here to the mouth. The exception is The Rapids at the base of Senatis Mountain between Rampart and Tanana. There are two wide channels along both banks that easily avoid the boulders in the middle of the river. The canyons between Rampart and Tanana can funnel wind to speeds that force a canoe to shore for days. And Big Bend, locally called Big Eddy, near the Kokrines Hills, can frequently be violently windy with waves to match. The river is now so wide that even moderate breezes have enough fetch to create waves capable of swamping an open boat.

Access/Towns: The only road access to this section is at Yukon Crossing. This is explained thoroughly in the previous section.

Galena has a bombproof runway built during World War II, with daily passenger service to Anchorage and Fairbanks. There is no need to make reservations with Frontier Flying Service, just sign your name on the first-come, first-served sign-up sheet. Northern Air Cargo flies large planes roughly twice weekly to Galena from Anchorage and Fairbanks that are easily capable of carrying canoes or kayaks. They only charge according to weight, not volume, so freight prices are downright low for the empty backhaul from the Bush to the big cities. All other villages in this section have passenger plane service, but the planes are too small to fly out boats.

Frontier Flying Service
(800) 478-6779
www.frontier-flying.com

Northern Air Cargo
(800) 727-214
www.nacargo.com

Maps: USGS 1:250:000 Quads:
Livengood
Tanana
Melozitna
Ruby
Nulato

Rest and Restocking: Rampart, Tanana, Ruby, and Galena line the banks of this section. Rampart is a very small village with only minimal services.

Tanana has a small café, two grocery stores, post office, and a number of bed and breakfasts. All of the services are visible or quickly accessible from the main beach.

At around 350 people, Ruby is on the small side. There is a quiet public beach, which, though rocky, is a good place to stay. A small store, post office, and washeteria round out the services. Ruby hosts a legendary Fourth of July celebration.

Galena is one of the largest villages on the Yukon River. There are two large grocery stores, café, washeteria, excellent plane service, bed and breakfasts, and comfortable, private camping on the beach.

Weather: Days can be warm in early July, and the weather doesn't generally change as quickly and violently as it does on the upper river. The wind seems to blow harder because the river is wider.

Section Discussion

As the Dalton Highway bridge fades behind the stern, you leave behind the last road crossing on the Yukon. The river is now the highway between villages. Skiff traffic will pick up past Rampart, with an average 5 to 15 boats passing daily. Most boat drivers will swing wide of your boat to keep their wake from rocking you, but a few don't know or care and will pass so close you have to scramble to turn and face the wake. Barges will occasionally pass, their football-field-size decks loaded with heavy equipment, lumber, and pallets of goods. Their wake is not much of a problem since they travel slowly and stick to the main channel. The few paddlers on the river from here to the mouth are committed to long distances and rely on themselves.

The Yukon is now a big river, averaging about a mile wide, but ranging up to 2 to 3 miles of fetch. In a small boat, it's best to start hugging shore, particularly when the wind picks up. It doesn't take much of a breeze to churn the Yukon into 5 or 6 foot waves in the current. The river still moves along in places, and depending on the wind and water level, 30 to 35 mile days should be a comfortable pace.

The last road crossing on the Yukon. The only way to leave the river over the next 800 miles is by plane. Paddlers from this point on are committed and independent.

Toward the end of June and during almost all of July, animals leave the river bottom and head into the surrounding green hills to feed. The islands through this stretch are relatively free of fresh moose and bear tracks at this time of year.

Yukon Crossing to Kallands

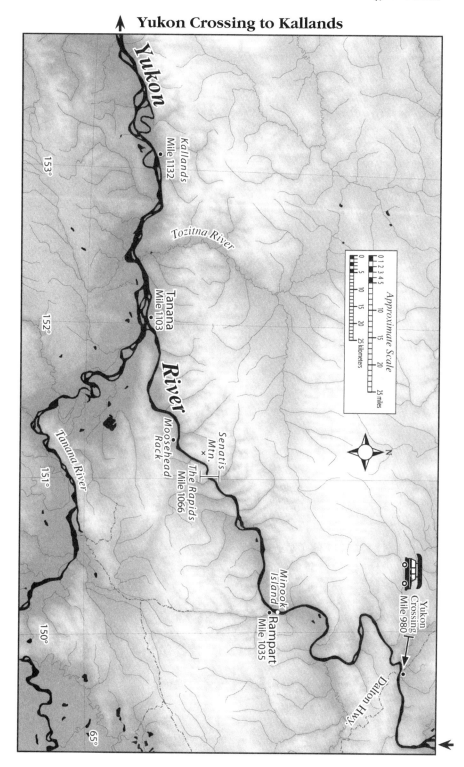

Yukon

Kallands
Mile 1132

Tozitna River

Tanana
Mile 1103

River

Tanana River

Moosehead
Rack

Senati's
Mtn.
×

The Rapids
Mile 1066

Minook
Island

Rampart
Mile 1035

Yukon
Crossing
Mile 980

Dalton Hwy.

153°

152°

151°

150°

65°

Approximate Scale

0 1 2 3 4 5

0   5   10   15   20   25 kilometers

0   5   10   15   20   25 miles

N

Kallands to Galena

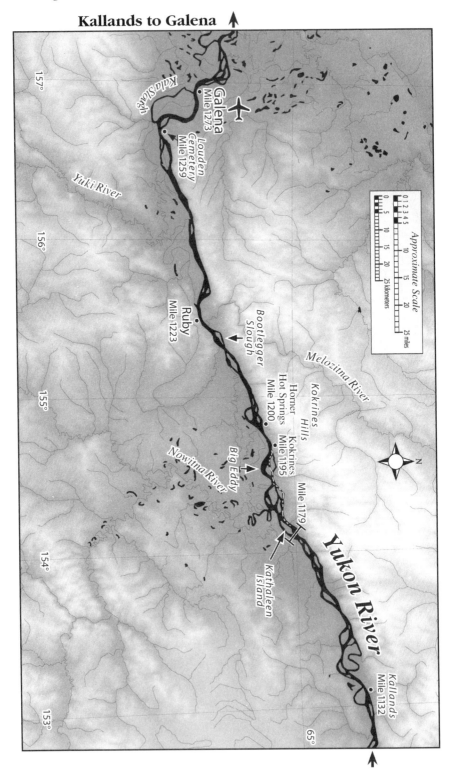

Significant Points

Mile 1035 (1666.7 km): Rampart, population 45, sits on the left bank. Around the turn of the century, this former mining town was one of the largest metropolitan areas in Alaska Territory. It was also the site of a short-lived state experimental farm for about a decade before World War I. There are frequent rumors of building a road from here to Fairbanks, but nothing has ever come of the project. The canyons above and below the village—roughly from Minook Island down past Moosehead Rack—act as a wind funnel and can force paddlers to shore to wait for the wind to die down. As always, bring plenty of food.

Mile 1066 (1716.6 km): The Rapids sit between cliffs on either side of the river. The current swirls around the rocks, and erupts in boiling eddies, churning the bottom. Many fish camps are crammed into this little valley to net salmon as they're thrown around in the current. The rocks in the middle of the channel are easy to avoid—just stick to either the left or right bank.

Mile 1103 (1776.2 km): The village of Tanana sits on the right bank just below the mouth of the Tanana River. Two groceries stores and the post office line the river and are plainly visible from the main beach. The washeteria is a few blocks due north.

Originally the site of large potlatches between Native tribes, Tanana still has an annual potlatch in June. Fort Gibbon and Fort Adams were established here in the late 1800s. After the forts shut down in the 1920s, Tanana has continued on because of its location at the hub of Alaska's two largest rivers.

With the addition of the Tanana River—the Yukon's largest tributary, in terms of both volumes of water and silt—the river is now truly huge. If you are not sticking closer to shore already, it is time to start being more conservative about heading into the middle of the channel. Many of the passages around islands are labeled "sloughs" on USGS maps, but unlike in the Flats, they are fine water to paddle through, both as shortcuts and to get out of the wind.

Mile 1132 (1811.2 km): Kallands is an abandoned wood cutting camp that serviced steamships. It is marked to provide geographic continuity between the two maps.

Mile 1179 (1898.6 km): Wind has an odd way of flowing off the Kokrines Hills, and Big Bend—called "Big Eddy" locally—is a nasty stretch of water when it is blowing. Seven or 8 foot waves with white caps are possible in the middle of the turn. Follow the dashed white line on the map to avoid the rough water.

When the wind is calm, the smell of rotting flesh can fill the air. The Yukon cuts through thick permafrost gravels here, and ice-age mammals frozen within the ground are frequently exposed. The smell is 10,000-year-old flesh finally rotting. Locals call the area "The Boneyard."

Mile 1195 (1912 km): Kokrines is an abandoned wood-cutting village that serviced steamboats. There are still a few cabins, a small cemetery, and lots of mosquitoes.

Mile 1200 (1932.4 km): Horner Hot Springs is a small group of private fish camps.

Mile 1223 (1969.4 km): The town of Ruby is the last village to sit on the left bank of the river. Nestled between two hills and falling steeply to the rocky beach, the village is visible from miles away. If you are following the right bank, paddle through Bootlegger Slough and cross the river in front of the village. Ruby sits in a naturally protected pocket on the river, and this route avoids the cliffs, currents, and waves on the main channel. Beach your boat above the line of skiffs to camp in a relatively untraveled part of town. Ruby has minimal services—small grocery store, washeteria, one bed and breakfast, and post office—but it is one of the most gorgeous locations on the whole river. If the timing works out, the town puts on an incredible Fourth of July celebration. The mouth of the Melozitna River directly across town contributes a mile long streak of clear water to the Yukon. This is a popular swimming and fishing spot for the village. A gravel road extends 50 miles into the hills south of town, servicing a few small placer mines and many, many mosquitoes.

Mile 1259 (2027 km): The brightly painted graves of Louden Cemetery watch the Yukon River flow by.

Mile 1273 (2049.5 km): You can hear Galena long before buildings appear: airplanes, four-wheelers, and chain saws seem to run around the clock. If you are planning to spend a few days here, make camp along the beach well before the public landing; it's quieter and much more private than the public beach, which has four-wheeler and boat traffic 24 hours a day. Bushwhack straight in from the river and you'll quickly reach the main road. Mark the spot with flagging so you can find it again.

A café with a public telephone sits right on the public beach, as well as a bed and breakfast. A small, but well-stocked grocery store is a block back from the public landing, and there are fuel, laundry, showers, a public phone, and a liquor store all in the same little complex as the store. Galena is a large village with roughly 800 people, and stores are open relatively late. A much larger grocery store is a mile or so east of the public landing along the main drag. This is a great place to stock up on food for the last leg of the trip to the delta.

An airport runway parallels the river and defines Galena. The airline offices are on the western end of the runway—just start walking on the road and someone will almost certainly give you a ride. Ask at the airport if you need a truck to haul gear and boats from the beach.

Run to the Delta

Distance: 520 miles (837.6 km)

Estimated Time: 18 to 21 days

Water Class/Hazards: Class I. Although the water is as smooth as a lake from Galena to the mouth, this section can be the most dangerous on the river. Storms are frequent and can churn calm water into 5 or 6 foot waves that easily swamp a canoe. It is almost guaranteed a storm will hit somewhere through here, forcing the paddler to shore to endure the weather for a few days. As always, carry more than enough food. Tides can be felt as far upriver as Holy Cross when the water surges forward during full moons or when the wind blows from the north or west. Always make camp and haul boats well up from shore.

Access: Any village along the river has small passenger plane service. Galena, described in the previous section, has excellent air service to the beginning of this stretch.
St. Marys, a few miles up the Andreafesky River, has excellent air service as well. Contact:
  Northern Air Cargo
  (800) 727-2171
  www.nacargo.com

  Hageland Aviation
  (passenger service)
  (866) 239-0119
  www.nacargo.com

Emmonak is the air hub of the Yukon Delta. Grant Aviation provides passenger service and Northern Air Cargo moves gear.
  Northern Air Cargo
  (800) 727-2171
  www.nacargo.com

  Grant Aviation
  (800) 478-1944
  www.flygrant.com

Arctic Transportation Service, Northern Air Cargo's agent in Emmonak, has a truck and will haul gear from the beach for a fee.

Maps: USGS 1:250:000
Nulato
Ophir
Unalakeet
Holy Cross
Russian Mission
Marshall
Kwiguk

Rest and Restocking: Load up on food in Galena grocery stores. St. Marys and Emmonak have the largest grocery stores downriver. Refer to the table in the introduction for the names of smaller villages.

Weather: The air gradually cools and gets wetter the closer the river gets to the Bering Sea. The last tall trees cling to the hills around Holy Cross, before giving way to low willows and cottonwoods that don't block the wind. Storms are frequent, violent, windy, rainy, and cold. Be conservative and pull over in a protected spot before the weather turns really ugly. Fog and drizzle are common, so expect all gear—including sleeping bags—to stay more or less soaked. A commercial-fishing-quality rain suit and rubber boots are indispensable.

Section Description

This is the final run to the sea. The 500 miles pass slowly as the current slackens and the wind, largely from the south, blows against the bow. Depending on the weather, 20 miles can be a very good day, although 25 will probably be an average. Stick close to the protected right bank and avoid crossing the river to get to villages. Count on getting pinned down on islands for at least a couple days when the weather turns foul. Mosquitoes become less of a problem closer to the ocean, and setting the tent up out of the wind in protected high willows starts to become more of a concern. Campsites turn muddy through here, and a patch of sand or gravel is a nice place to land to save slogging through knee-deep mud. Be careful. Test the ground before putting your full weight on it. There are some patches of dangerous quick mud, especially around the mouth of the Koyukuk River.

Salmon runs are especially thick near the ocean, and there are many fish camps, set nets, fish wheels, and people in skiffs tending drift nets. Orange buoys mark the set nets, and it is wise to swing a little wide of them because nets are set in swirling current, which can knock boats around. Villages pass by sometimes once a day—it feels almost densely populated.

The salmon attract both people and bears. From Kaltag to Russian Mission it will be a slow day if only five black bears wander the banks. It is especially important to always camp on islands through here. And make sure you don't camp near the mouths of tributaries, since they have unusually dense bear populations. If a bear does come into camp, making a loud noise can usually scare them off—these are wild bears and are generally afraid of people.

It is illegal to possess alcohol from Last Chance, just past the village of Koyukuk, to the mouth.

Strangers are quite rare through this section of the river, so you will stand out. Don't be shy about introducing yourself and explaining why you're there. Most villagers are friendly. Just remember: you are the curiosity.

Galena to Bullfrog Island

65°

Koyukuk River

Koyukuk
Mile 1305

Koyukuk Island

Last Chance
Mile 1307

Yistletaw
(Bishops Rock)
Mile 1293

Pilot Sl.

Galena
Mile 1273

Nulato
Mile 1323

Pilot Mtn.

Kala Sl.

Ninemile Island

Halfway Island

Kaltag
Mile 1357

Kaltag Portage

N

Yukon River

Big Eightmile Island

64°

Approximate Scale

0 1 2 3 4 5   10   15   20   25 miles

0   5   10   15   20   25 kilometers

Bullfrog Island

159°   158°   157°

Bullfrog Island to Paimut

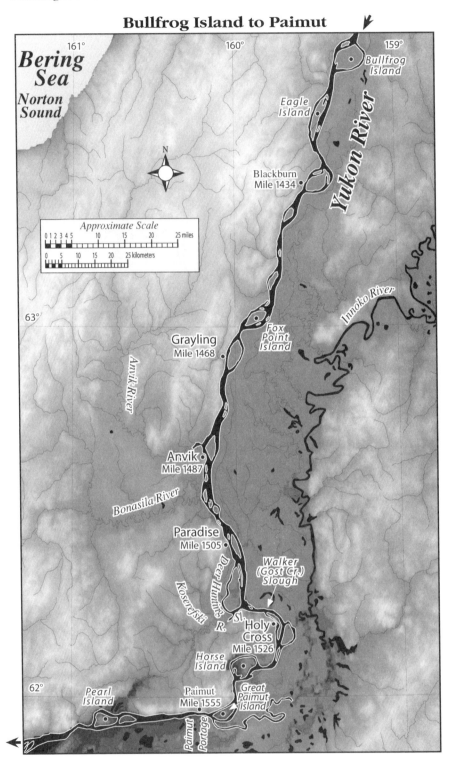

Bering Sea
Norton Sound

161°   160°   159°

Bullfrog Island

Yukon River

Eagle Island

N

Blackburn
Mile 1434

Approximate Scale
0 1 2 3 4 5   10   15   20   25 miles
0   5   10   15   20   25 kilometers

Innoko River

63°

Fox
Point
Island

Grayling
Mile 1468

Anvik River

Anvik
Mile 1487

Bonasila River

Paradise
Mile 1505

Walker
(Gost Cr.)
Slough

Koserefski R.

Deer Hunting Slough

Holy
Cross
Mile 1526

Horse
Island

62°

Pearl
Island

Paimut
Mile 1555

Great
Paimut
Island

Paimut
Portage

Paimut to Mountain Village

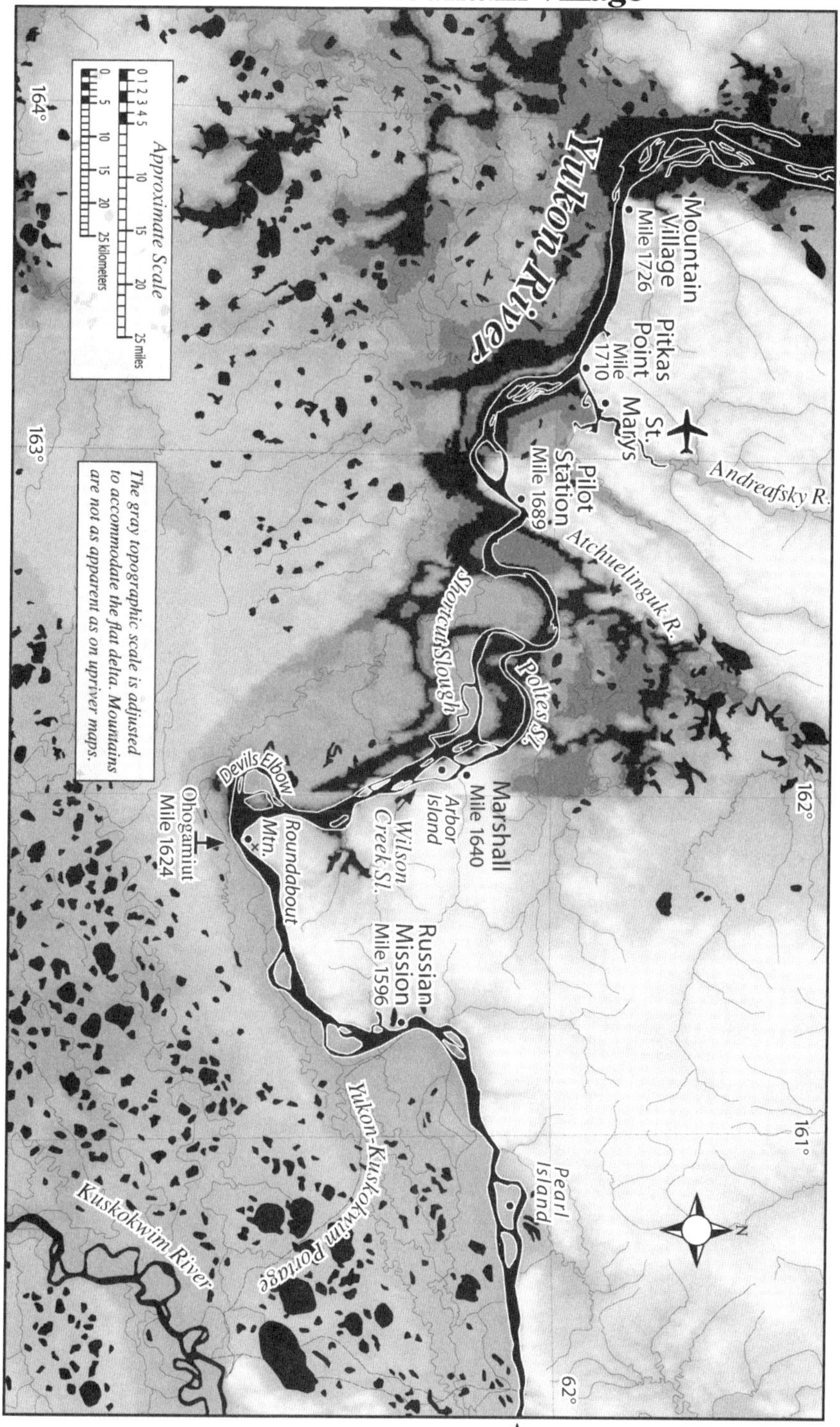

Approximate Scale

0 1 2 3 4 5

0 5 10 15 20 25 kilometers

25 miles

The gray topographic scale is adjusted to accommodate the flat delta. Mountains are not as apparent as on upriver maps.

164°

163°

Yukon River

Mountain Village
Mile 1726

Pitkas Point
Mile 1710

St. Marys

Pilot Station
Mile 1689

Andreafsky R.

Atchuelinguk R.

Shageluk Slough

Pollerz Sl.

162°

Devils Elbow

Ohogamiut
Mile 1624

Roundabout

Mtn.

Arbor Island

Marshall
Mile 1640

Wilson Creek Sl.

Russian Mission
Mile 1596

Yukon-Kuskokwim Portage

Pearl Island

161°

62°

Kuskokwim River

N

Mountain Village to Emmonak

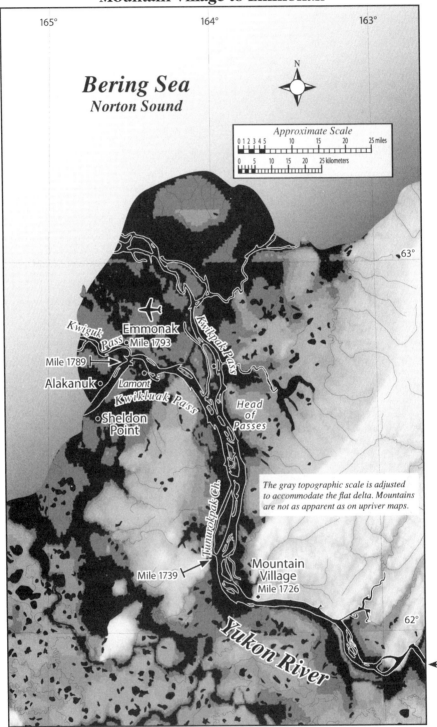

The gray topographic scale is adjusted to accommodate the flat delta. Mountains are not as apparent as on upriver maps.

Significant Points

Mile 1293 (2082.1 km): Yistletaw is collection of fish camps. Nets are strung at the base of the Bishop Rock in the swirling eddies and fish are filleted and smoked in the camp. Locally, people call the camp Bishop Rock and if you use the name Yistletaw you'll get a look of incomprehension.

Frank Fuller, a lay Catholic volunteer, murdered Bishop John Seghers while traveling through here in 1886. Hence, the name of the camp and rock.

Mile 1305 (2101.4 km): Koyukuk is a small village at the mouth of the Koyukuk River, the third largest tributary to the Yukon. It serves as the last location on the Yukon before turning up the 500-mile long Koyukuk River, covered in a different section of this book. Except for the many sloughs, islands, and mud bars through here, it is hard to tell a major river joins the flow. Some of these islands have quick mud shores. Test the footing carefully before stepping out of the boat.

Mile 1307 (2104.3 km): Last Chance is a cabin and liquor store on the right. Below this point alcohol is illegal.

Mile 1323 (2130.4 km): Nulato is a village of 300 people. Founded as a

Nulato has not grown a great deal since this 1899 view.
(*Jaspar Wyman Collection, Anchorage Museum*)

fur trading post by the Russian American Company in the early 1800s, it is also the site of the Nulato Massacre. Koyukon chief and medicine man Lolee-ann attacked the post in February, 1851. Retaliating against disrespectful treatment—the post commander lived with two of Lolee-ann's daughters and an English visitor imperiously "sent for" him—he led a small group of followers as they burned alive around 100 Nulato people inside their winter cabins before attacking the fort and knifing the offending foreigners. Afterwards, the Russian American Company sent gifts and ended one of the only armed conflicts between Natives and Europeans in Alaska.

Mile 1357 (2185.2 km): Kaltag is a village of roughly 200 people. It sits on the inland side of the Kaltag Portage, a winter trail over the hills to the Bering Sea village of Unalakeet. The Portage is impassable muskeg, mosquitoes, and brown bears in summer.

Mile 1434 (2309.2 km): Blackburn is an informal collection of cabins.

Mile 1468 (2363.4 km): Grayling is another small village, with roughly 200 people. This community was founded in 1962 when 25 families moved from the frequently flooded village of Holikachuk on the Innoko River. Grayling Creek has incredible fishing, and that's how the village got its name.

Mile 1487 (2394.5 km): Anvik is set back from the river in a protected slough easily visible from the main channel. Roughly 100 people live in this community. White traders found a rare settled Athabascan village when they visited in 1834. An Episcopalian mission and orphanage were established in 1887. Villagers today rely on a mix of subsistence fishing and seasonal jobs.

Mile 1505 (2423.5 km): Paradise doesn't exist. Is this saying something profound?

Mile 1526 (2457.3 km): Stick close to the right bank well above the village, and turn into Walker Slough (called Gost Creek Slough locally) to reach Holy Cross. The area is thick with fish camps. Deer Hunting Slough and the sandbars at the mouth of the Koserefski River are usually covered with spawned-out, dead salmon and tons of black bears. Choose campsites with extra care from here to Russian Mission. Occasional tidal surges can reach this far upriver. All the villages marked on the USGS map between Holy Cross and Russian Mission are now fish camps.

Holy Cross was founded as a Roman Catholic mission in 1886, directly on the banks of the Yukon River. The slough began forming in the 1930s, gradually cutting off the community from the main river. Now, in low-water years, barges cannot reach the village. The mission closed in the 1950s, and the 300 villagers moved onto the former mission land.

The mission that founded Holy Cross is no longer there. Once open to the main channel, a shallow slough now leads to the village. (Jaspar Wyman Collection, Anchorage Museum)

Mile 1555 (2503.6 km): The Paimut Portage—and the Yukon Kuskokwim Portage directly across from Russian Mission—is a series of winter trails through swamps and across lakes to the nearby Kuskokwim River. They are impassable in summer. Paimut is a former village, abandoned by the 1950s.

Mile 1596 (2569.6 km): Russian Mission has two small stores. The beach is extremely muddy and there are no other visitor facilities. As you might guess from the name, Russian Mission was named by Russian Orthodox missionaries, but it was founded as a Russian trading post in 1837. The onion domes, place names, and people's names from here to the mouth all reflect the strong influence of the Russians who lived here from the late 1700s to mid 1800s. *Gussak,* the Native word for a white person, is probably derived from the Russian *Cossack.*

Mile 1624 (2615.1 km): Ohogamiut is an abandoned village presently used as a fish camp. This is a nasty place to get caught in a storm. The bending river boils up strange currents and there are few places to pull to shore along the bluffs. Take the inside channel to avoid Devils Elbow. Be very cautious paddling through here: if the weather seems even slightly bad, just pull over and camp until it blows past.

Mile 1640 (2640.9 km): It is possible to access Marshall from Wilson Creek Slough or by crossing directly in front of the village along Arbor

Island. If you stop in Marshall, you'll have to follow Poltes Slough back to the main channel, but it is just as sluggish and exposed to the wind as the main river. Short Cut Slough—the entrance is directly across from Marshall—avoids the wind but watch for speeding skiffs in the narrow, winding channel.

Marshall is now a largely Native village, but it was founded to provide river access to the gold mines in the surrounding hills.

Mile 1689 (2719.8 km): Pilot Station, an old steamboat staging town, sits nestled between rocky bluffs below the mouth of the Atchuelin-guk River. The merging currents just above town can get whipped into dangerous waves by sudden gusts rolling down the Atchuelinguk valley. The safest place to cross is directly in front of the beach.

Mile 1710 (2753.6 km): Pitkas Point is a good landing spot to walk the 3 miles to St. Marys if paddling up the sluggish Andreafsky River is out of the question. If you intend to stop in St. Marys or Mountain Village, it's best to stick to the right bank all the way from Pilot Station to avoid crossing the river. From here almost to the mouth, the river is 2 to 4 miles wide and a crossing is something to be avoided.

St. Marys is the largest village on this stretch of the Yukon and has a full set of services. Many people end their Yukon trip here—it skips the wide flat water on the delta. Washeterias now have not just washing machines and showers, but public saunas, too. It is a mark of pride to outlast other people in the steam. You will not be able to keep up with the locals. Past Pitkas Point, there is very little usable firewood on the islands and gravel bars. Make sure to have plenty of stove fuel for this stretch.

Mile 1726 (2779.4 km): Mountain Village is the last community before the delta flats. During the summer, the wind comes mostly from the south, so the left bank can be the lee. If you've stopped at any of the villages along the hills here, you may have a dangerous river crossing ahead. The bend after Mountain Village is filled with more sandbars and islands than the map shows, and this can be a more protected place to cross than in front of the villages.

Mile 1739 (2800.3 km): Tunurokpak Channel provides a route out of the wind and waves off the main river. But by paddling here you trade the hazard of open water for the danger of speeding skiffs in a narrow channel.

Mile 1789 (2880.8 km): The entrance to Kwiguk Pass, where Emmonak sits, is a potential bad spot. Weird currents boil unexpectedly on the upstream side, so it works best to swing a little wide as you make the turn into the channel. If it's stormy, wait for the weather to settle before making the crossing. It isn't necessary to start crossing until you reach the point past the geographic location of Lamont.

Mile 1793 (2887.3 km): Emmonak! You've done a great thing. But Emmonak isn't quite on the Bering Sea—it sits in the shelter of a river bend about 11 miles back from the exposed ocean. Going this last little bit is tricky. There are a couple choices. The hardcore method is to paddle to the sea, then time the tides to ride the incoming water back to Emmonak. Or, you can meet someone with a skiff on the beach and pay them a little to pick you up after you paddle to the ocean. Or, you can make the whole round-trip in a skiff. A surprisingly high percentage of people who paddle the Yukon River this far do not cover the last few miles to salt water in any manner. There are probably as many reasons for this as there are paddlers.

Emmonak, the bittersweet end.

Now you have to get back home. The little island in front of the store is a more private place to stay than the narrow, rocky beach. You can travel between camp and village in your empty boat. The washeteria is open only every other day, but there is a café and well-stocked grocery store. Emmonak has an almost cosmopolitan feel after the interior villages since it attracts people from all over Alaska and the United States to work the fertile commercial fishing here.

Selling a boat is tough—notice all the kayaks and canoes in villagers' yards. It is possible to put a classified ad on the local cable television system or you can put a notice card in the arctic entry to the Alaska Commercial store. Don't expect much more than a symbolic payment. Airfreight rates back to Anchorage are quite reasonable, and if you want to sell the boat, you might have better luck there and can certainly get a better price if you do sell it.

Ta da!

Tanana River

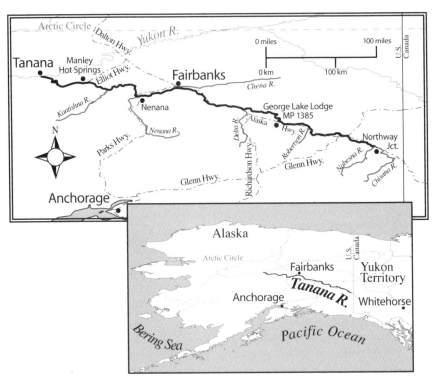

The Tanana River is the most suitable river in this book for short trips. The frequent highway and road crossings make any length trip possible from an afternoon jaunt, to a long weekend, to a three-week journey completing the river. This is a great watery path for visitors traveling the Alaska Highway who want to stop for some short paddles, or people from Fairbanks looking for a way to spend a weekend. But, for a variety of reasons, the Tanana is uncommonly paddled above Fairbanks and below Nenana.

The Tanana is the Yukon's largest tributary in almost every hydrologic respect: longest channel, heaviest sediment load, and the most water. As might be expected from such a large river, it changes character many times. The upper stretch is a gentle current, floating in a single channel through muddy banks. From the Robertson River to just above Fairbanks, the Tanana is swift, heavily braided, and should be floated only by experienced paddlers. Below Fairbanks, the Tanana takes on the characteristics of a major regional river, slowing and widening to the point that barges can share the river with plenty of room to spare. There are numerous fish camps, with fish wheels catching salmon and whitefish.

This channel through the Interior was used as the region's highway until the 1950s. Blacktop highway construction in the 1940s and 1950s grounded steamboats and smaller freight craft. Today, barge traffic is only plentiful below Nenana, a port city whose primary reason for existence is loading freight for the roadless Interior. Almost all other uses of the river are recreational.

Tanana River Guide
Planning the Paddle

Where does the Tanana begin and end?

The start of the Tanana is remarkably straightforward: the Chisana and Nebesna Rivers, really two muddy creeks, meet in a swamp past Northway Junction to create the Tanana. After flowing nearly 600 miles through swamps, beneath towering glaciated peaks, and through wide valleys, it finally spills into the Yukon River in a 2 mile-wide channel.

Paddling Skills

There are three main parts to the Tanana: the single channel upper river, the heavily braided and swift middle stretch, and the wide, lazy river from Fairbanks to the mouth at the Yukon.

The upper river from the start to the mouth of the Robertson, and the lower river from Fairbanks to the Yukon, are flat, smooth stretches suitable for many paddling abilities. The most dangerous thing through here is speeding skiffs. For whatever reason, the Tanana attracts a particularly inconsiderate breed of motor boat operators. To a boat, they will not give you any room as they pass, nor will they slow down to reduce their wake. When you see a skiff, expect it to pass within feet of you at high speed.

The Alaska Range blends with the clouds over Goodpastor Flats. The jumbled driftwood and gravel bars are the hallmarks of braided rivers.

From the Robertson River mouth to just above Fairbanks, roughly 200 miles, the Tanana is swift, and heavily braided with gravel bars and snag mounds, rushing by tundra-covered peaks. There are no bouldery rapids through here—the water is technically Class I to II—but the speed, sediment load, numerous snags, and shifting channels make this water substantially more difficult to paddle than the class rating implies. Only experienced paddlers should do this stretch. Besides the spectacular scenery, this water has the additional advantage of discouraging skiffs, and there are very few motorboats, offering a fair degree of road-accessible isolation—something that is increasingly rare.

Timing

The Tanana is generally fast. If you paddle between the end of June and the beginning of September, the entire river is comfortably floatable in two and a half to three easy weeks. Some of the shorter section's rough trip times are: Northway Junction to the Alaska Highway bridge, two and a half days; Alaska Highway bridge to George Lake Lodge (MP1385), three days; George Lake Lodge (MP1385) to Delta Junction, one and a half days; Delta Junction to Fairbanks (Chena Pump Road put-in), two days; Fairbanks to Nenana, a day and a half; Nenana to Manley Hot Springs, four days; Manley to Tanana village, two to three days.

Boat Type

Canoe or kayak, choose your poison. Neither boat type has overwhelming practical advantages over the other—although canoes can be nice on the braided stretches since they are easy to hop in and out of when you ground on a gravel bar. Catarafts would also be okay on the braided stretches; packable boats are fine on single channels.

Weather and Water

The Interior can be downright warm in June and July, with temperatures routinely in the 70s. It is usually dry then, too, with the odd violent thunderstorm. August is usually rainy and cool. In September, fall starts to arrive, although in the early part of the month, there are usually some gorgeous, warm, sunny days followed by cold nights after the leaves and tundra have started turning colors. This is a particularly delightful time of year.

The Tanana is generally ice free from the end of May to the end of September. The Tanana flows north, so spring flooding as the headwaters melt before the mouth is frequent, serious, and something to be avoided. Waiting until the end of May before setting out will avoid almost all problem ice.

The Tanana River is fed primarily from glacial meltwater, and has different, counter-intuitive flow dynamics compared with rivers fed primarily by snowmelt or rain. As the chart below clearly shows, the warmer the weather, the higher the river. As glacial ice melts, the water rushes out through dusty, gravelly riverbeds. So not only is there more water in the channel when it's hot, there is also substantially more sediment.

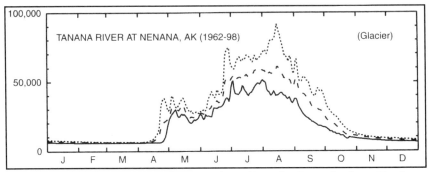

Reproduced with permission from Brabets, Timothy P. and others, Environmental and Hydrologic Overview of the Yukon River Basin, Alaska and Canada. Water Resources Investigations Report 99-4202, US Geological Survey, Anchorage, AK, 2000.

Drinking Water

All those glaciers grind the surrounding mountains and wash the dirt into the river making the Tanana downright gritty. Any random gallon will plug a water filter in just a few strokes of the pump. The only way to make drinking water is to let it sit overnight so the sediment can settle to the bottom.

Fairbanks discharges treated sewage into the Tanana. Before passing Alaska's second largest city, you might want to stock up on at least a day's worth of water so everything has a chance to settle out. Regardless, below Fairbanks you should be much more conscientious about treating water than above.

Gear

One of the nicest things about the Tanana is that the frequent road accesses make arranging boats and food the easiest of any river in Alaska. Fairbanks has a number of stores that rent boats and paddles, or you can drive your own boat to any number of put-ins along the way.

Maps

The USGS 1:250,000 maps are:
  Tanacross
  Mt. Hayes

Big Delta
Fairbanks
Kantishna River
Tanana

Rest and Resupply Points

Paved roads parallel the upper 5/7 of the Tanana, and there are numerous informal access points to the Tanana River off the highways and residential areas. This guide is only concerned with the public places a visitor can easily find.

River Mile/km	Town & Zip Code	Road	Cargo Plane	Grocery Store	Café
0	Northway • 99764	✓			✓ •
115/185.2	Tanacross 99776	✓			
201/323.6	George Lake Lodge • •*	✓			
267/429.9	Big Delta • •**	✓			✓
368/592.5	Fairbanks 99701	✓	✓	✓	✓
420/676.2	Nenana 99760	✓		✓	✓
527/848.5	Manly Hot Springs 99756 • •	✓			

• Northway is very dispersed. A RV campground, gas station, and well-stocked convenience store are at the junction of the Alaska Highway and the Northway Spur Road. Several hundred yards down the spur road is the unimproved public access to the Chisana River. The Chisana quickly flows into the Tanana. It is money well spent to leave your vehicle at the RV campground rather than at the put-in. The café, along with bar and motel, is actually a further 6 miles down the Northway Spur Road to the Northway Airport.

• • No PO

*George Lake Lodge is no longer. There is still paved access off the Alaska Highway at milepost 1385 (MP 1385), and parking.

**Big Delta, though not really a town, is full of services for paddlers.

Manley Hot Springs is actually 2.5 miles up the dirt road from Hot Springs Slough.

Tanana River Guide

Northway Crossing to George Lake Lodge (MP 1385)

Miles: 201 miles/323.6 km from the Northway put-in to the George Lake Lodge (MP 1385) take-out

Water Class: I-II

Estimated Time: 5 to 7 days

Access: This section is road accessible at four points:
The public put-in on the Chisana River on the Northway Road.
The Alaska Highway bridge between Tok and the Taylor Highway.
The community of Tanacross.
The Alaska Highway crossing of the Robertson River.
Alaska Highway MP 1385 access to the Tanana. There is a historical sign discussing the impact of the gold rush on Natives. This spot is marked George Lake Lodge on USGS maps, but the lodge no longer exists.

Outfitters: None. The best source of paddling gear and other supplies is in Fairbanks, 385 road miles from Northway. Tok has a small, decent grocery store, plus there are convenience stores at Northway and Tanacross.

Rest and Restocking: None.

Maps: USGS 1:250:000
Tanacross
Mt. Hayes

Section Description

This flat water, road-accessible portion of the Tanana is perhaps one of the best places in Alaska to learn multiday river paddling. The frequent access points provide a great deal of flexibility, with anywhere from a weekend to a week-long paddle possible. The channel is relatively narrow, so wind-churned waves are not much of a problem. Plus, the channel is largely clear of obstructions. The only drawbacks to this section are the road noise from the sparsely traveled Alaska Highway and the challenge of finding a well-drained camp spot above the Robertson River mouth. As a bonus, the Alaska Range towers over the water. Furthermore, the Tanana between the Robertson River and George Lake Lodge (MP 1385) provides an excellent introduction to paddling braided rivers, since the gravel bars are relatively easy to navigate, short, and there is a nearby road in case you really get in trouble on the river.

Northway Crossing to George Lake Lodge (MP 1385)

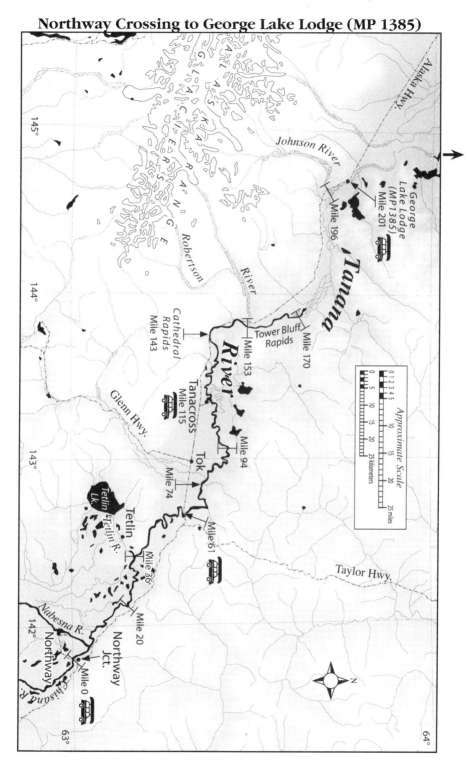

Cathedral Rapids lies just around the next bend.

Significant Points

Mile 0: The Chisana River put-in on the Northway road is less than a mile from the Alaska Highway. It is a wise use of money to park your vehicle at the Naabia Niign Campground/RV park by the highway turnoff rather than leaving it parked at the access. It is a short walk down the road between the two points.

The Chisana River is a gently flowing creek winding through swampland. Within 4 miles, the Nabesna River joins the flow, and the river is now officially the Tanana. The river winds along through swamps, maintaining the same character for the next 60 or so miles. Dry ground campsites are rare through here. The upriver portions of mudbars and islands are usually much sandier than the downstream sections. Although they are harder to line up on in a current, the upriver portions are usually the only ground capable of supporting a camp.

Mile 20 (32.3 km): The river briefly bends almost to the Alaska Highway by the old Riverside Lodge, but there is no public river access or lodge here.

Mile 36 (58.0 km): The mouth of the Tetlin River. The village of Tetlin, 5 miles upstream, has about 100 residents. Most people you see in skiffs on this section are from Tetlin.

Mile 61 (98.2 km): The Alaska Highway bridge crossing. There is parking and river access on the left bank. If using this spot as a takeout, you would be better off not parking here overnight; instead, leave your vehicle in Tok and make some sort of ride arrangement or hitchhike the 12 miles between the two places.

The Alaska Highway bridge between Tok and Northway. With numerous crossings, the Tanana is the most easily road accessible river in this book.

Mile 74 (119.1 km): The USGS map shows a dirt road leading from Tok to this point in the Tanana. There are private homes at the end of this road and no public access.

Mile 94 (151.3 km): The river flows along the base of towering cliffs, hinting at the change in scenery to come.

Mile 115 (185.2 km): Tanacross is largely a Native village of roughly 110. The cabins on the right bank are what was left after the old village burned in a forest fire in 1979. The present village is on the left bank, down a short spur road from the highway. There is a major landing strip just upstream of town, which is used in the summer as a forest-fire-fighting base. The town itself is fairly small, with a small convenience store and public-use telephone the only services for travelers. Although the road comes down to the river at many put-ins, it is not recommended to leave your vehicle there overnight unless you know people in Tanacross and can leave it at a friend's house.

Tanacross was founded around the turn of the century as the site of an Episcopal mission church called St. Timothy's. The name of the community bounced between St. Timothy's and Tanana Crossing, until finally settling on Tanacross to emphasize the town's position on a slack-water river crossing.

Mile 143 (230.2 km): After the spectacular approach to the mountains shown in the introduction to this section, the river takes a sharp right turn and flows through Cathedral Rapids. Cathedral Riffle would be a more accurate name. Experienced paddlers paying attention will have no trouble navigating the Class I to II chop. There is much rougher and more difficult water to paddle ahead in unnamed areas of the river.

The USGS map shows a number of cabins here, but there are no longer any buildings.

Mile 153 (246.3 km): The Robertson River seems to pour more gravel than water into the Tanana. The Tower Bluff Rapids downstream from the Robertson mouth is a forgiving place to get a first taste of paddling braided water. The water is flat Class I to II, the braided section is only about 3 miles, and the Alaska Highway is close by in case you get in trouble.

Paddling Braided Rivers Sidebar

As you paddle a braided river, try to pick the widest channel that holds to the middle of the river. It is always best to paddle with bare gravel bars on both banks. However, if given a choice between a channel lined with cottonwoods or one lined with black spruce, follow the cottonwood channel; eroding banks undercut black spruces, leaving them leaning across the water as sweepers. Cottonwoods and poplars have a much weaker root system and are more likely to wash away from the bank. Also, when you inevitably ground the boat on a shallow gravel bar, hop out on the upstream side. As you push the boat across the rocks, always keep a firm grip on it. And test the water depth before committing your foot to a forward step; the current frequently cuts bars off abruptly.

Mile 170 (272 km): The river splits into many fine channels without landmarks. Just try to follow the widest, deepest water away from black spruce-lined banks.

Mile 196 (315.6 km): The Johnson River flows into the Tanana just past an unnamed hill and the channel becomes heavily braided again. If you are pulling out at the old George Lake Lodge (MP 1385) access, start sticking to the left channel as much as possible

Mile 201 (323.6 km): The George Lake Lodge (MP 1385) access is on a wide channel and conscientious paddlers will have no trouble spotting it. However, the current is fairly swift through here, so start paddling for shore as soon as you spot it.

George Lake Lodge (MP1385) to Fairbanks

Miles: 167 miles/ 268.9 km

Water Class: I-II. The water class rating here is deceptively low. The river is heavily braided, swift, and there are numerous sweepers that need to be avoided by skillful, experienced route picking. Boiling eddies fill the channel in places. *This stretch is recommended only for expert paddlers.*

Estimated Time: 5 to 7 days

Access: There are six major road access points, some on tributary streams:
> The old George Lake Lodge (MP1385)
> Big Delta Richardson Highway crossing
> Shaw Creek Boat Launch
> Salcha River State Recreation Site/Boat Launch
> Chena River in Fairbanks
> Chena Pump Road Public Access

Outfitters: None directly on the river. Beaver Sports in Fairbanks rents and sells boats and paddling accessories:

Beaver Sports	Alaska Outdoor Rental & Guides
3480 College Road	P.O. Box 82388
Fairbanks, AK 99709	Fairbanks, AK 99708
(907)479-2494	Phone: (907) 457-2453
www.beaversports.com	Email: larryk@akbike.com
	Web:www.akbike.com
	They are on located on the banks of the Chena River at Paddler's Cove at Pioneer Park (nee Alaskaland).

Rest and Restocking: Rika's Roadhouse has a restaurant, telephone, and restored roadhouse.
Fairbanks has all the amenities and services of a midsize city, although it is difficult to get to from the Tanana.

Maps: USGS 1:250:000
> Mt. Hayes
> Big Delta
> Fairbanks

Section Description
This stretch is swift, heavily braided, wide, and windy. The water

moves so quickly most paddling effort is put only into steering. An experienced, alert drifter will enjoy this section thoroughly; it is easily one of the most enjoyable paddles of any in this book. The choice of excellent campsites is almost infinite. The mountains towering above the river are distracting and lovely. There a number of road access points.

It can be a little tough to find the water on the braided stretches of the Tanana.

And, it is possible to do any length from a day to a week. However, *a beginner can get in a lot of trouble and should not travel this section.* The stretch between Tanacross and George Lake Lodge (MP1385) is a much more forgiving place to learn to paddle braided rivers.

George Lake Lodge (MP1385) to Fairbanks

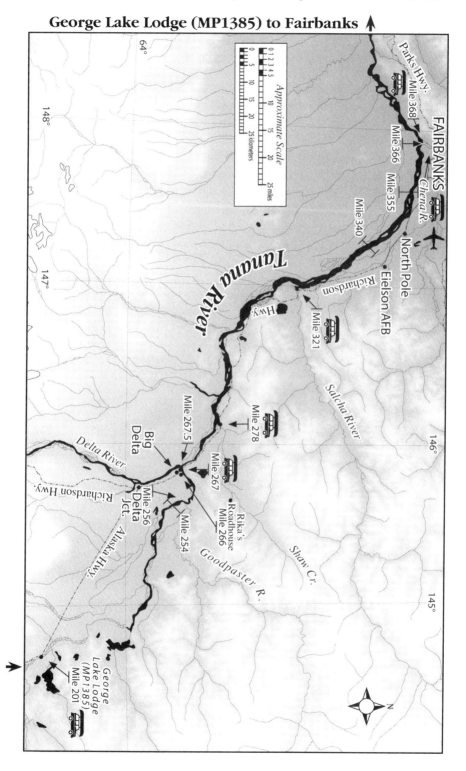

Significant Points

Mile 201 (323.6 km): From the old George Lake Lodge (MP1385) put-in to the end of the Clearwater/Goodpastor Flats, a distance of 50 miles, the river is almost continuously braided. The current is swift, the channels are many, and there can be sweepers, snag piles, and dead-end channels. These obstacles change from year to year and it is up to you to navigate them safely. There are also a number of boiling eddies which fill the entire channel. They should not cause any problems, provided the weather is calm and the paddler methodically works the boat forward.

Mile 254 (408.9 km): The channel is no longer so heavily braided and is cut by muddier islands.

Mile 256 (412.2 km): Bluff Cabin is on the left bank beneath a large bluff, appropriately enough. The cabin is abandoned, with a decent roof and a hole in the ground from the old root cellar. There is a four-wheeler trail between town and the cabin and it is an occasional party spot for teenagers.

Mile 266 (428.3 km): Rika's Roadhouse is a restored roadhouse plainly visible and easily accessed from the river. A very small clear creek flows in from a cutbank from the top of the clearing—your moored boat is well hidden from land view here. Take a left to reach the state park campground, go right for the café, which also has a telephone, and the roadhouse. Besides the welcome food, plan on spending a few hours poking around the restored buildings: there is a telegraph station, barracks, and garden, too. But paddlers will have an appreciation deeper than the average visitor as they gaze upon the old riverboat. You think it's tricky picking routes you won't ground on in your shallow draft boat—just imagine what's it like to pilot a boat 40 feet long through the river you just came through.

There is a gas station and convenience store directly across the Richardson Highway from the roadhouse as well as public access and parking to the Tanana and Delta Rivers.

Mile 267 (429.9 km): The Richardson Highway and the trans-Alaska pipeline cross the river. There are popular public access parking areas on the left bank.

Mile 267.5 (430.7 km): The Delta River joins the Tanana. Watch for swirling currents along the bluff on the right bank. Watch for strong winds coming off the Delta River. The current picks up speed and a tremendous gravel load, too. *This stretch of the Tanana, from the*

Delta River mouth to Fairbanks is extremely challenging water and should be traveled only by expert braided river paddlers. The channel is wide—up to 3 miles—and places a premium on route-picking skills. In a few places the current is strong enough to create standing waves, but there are no large rocks blocking any channels, just snags, sweepers, and gravel bars. The area can be tremendously windy and paddlers should plan food accordingly; you may have to wait a few days for the wind to subside enough to resume travel.

Mile 278 (447.6 km): A public access at Shaw Creek provides quick access to the Tanana.

Mile 321 (516.8 km): The Salcha River imperceptibly joins the flow. The Salcha River State Recreation Area has a boat launch with a short jaunt down the tributary to the Tanana. Watch for inconsiderate skiff drivers.

At roughly this point, military planes from nearby Eielson Air Force Base will begin to fill the sky. This is either cool to watch or annoying to listen to, depending on your attitude. If you are paddling beyond Fairbanks, it might be a good idea to stock up on enough water to get a day or two beyond the treated sewage outflow of Alaska's second-largest city.

Mile 340 (547.4 km) (roughly) : The cracking towers of the North Pole refinery begin showing above the trees. They will be visible for several hours.

Mile 355 (571.6 km) (roughly): The channel begins to consolidate, slow, and turn muddier as the river begins its big bend. From here to the Chena River mouth, there is mile after mile of riprap fencing for flood and erosion prevention. There is no formal public access to Fairbanks from this stretch, although there are numerous informal tracks, roads, and paths. You will probably hear gunshots from illegal shooting areas. There is a fair amount of trash dumping. And a dragline or two mines gravel from the riverbed. This is definitely not the view of Alaska's second-largest city normally presented in tourist brochures. While paddling, it is plain to see that Fairbanks is built as far upriver on the Tanana as a large steamship is capable of traveling.

Mile 366 (589.3 km): The Chena River sluggishly joins the Tanana. The Chena flows through the heart of Fairbanks and there are too many accesses on it to mention. However, the Chena River State Park in the middle of town provides not only cheap camping—$10 a night for tents—but also a nice put-in and slow paddle through town. The emphasis is on *slow*. The Chena hardly moves. And watch out for speeding skiffs. But it is a cheap and easy place to base a trip from if you are from out of town.

Mile 366.25 (589.7 km): Just past the mouth of the Chena is a strange sight: a recreated Bush village and fish camp. This is part of the River Boat Discovery Tour, a diesel-powered paddleboat which travels the Chena and Tanana showing passengers recreations of certain aspects of Bush life. Keep paddling to the Yukon and you will see the real thing.

Mile 368 (592.5 km): Chena Pump public access. There is no phone or facilities beyond an outhouse, picnic shelter, and parking spaces here. However, this is the best boat launch from a road to the Tanana in Fairbanks. There are no services within a quick walk and it is several miles down the road to the nearest public phone. Cell phones work well in Fairbanks, and carrying one would be especially handy to arrange a pickup here.

Tanana River Guide

Fairbanks to the Yukon River

Miles: 227 miles / 365.5 km

Water Class: I

Estimated Time: 7 to 9 days

Access: Chena Pump Public Access
Nenana City dock
Manly Hot Springs

Outfitters: None

Rest and Restocking: Nenana has a café, motels, and well-stocked grocery. Manly Hot Springs has a café, motel, and hot springs.

Maps: USGS 1:250:000
Fairbanks
Kantishna River
Tanana

Section Description

The Tanana undergoes a dramatic character change past Fairbanks. It is now wide, split by large islands, and more sluggish. There are the first hints of life in the Bush: fish camps line the river and barges churn by, loaded with material for Yukon villagers. The paddle is gentle and a relaxing change of pace after the nonstop concentration required on the braided upper river. It is possible to cut off most of the big oxbows by following side channels, and progress is relatively fast.

Don't forget to stop and relax in your headlong rush to finish a trip. Some of my most pleasant memories are days spent in camp, napping, and reading books.

Fairbanks to the Yukon River

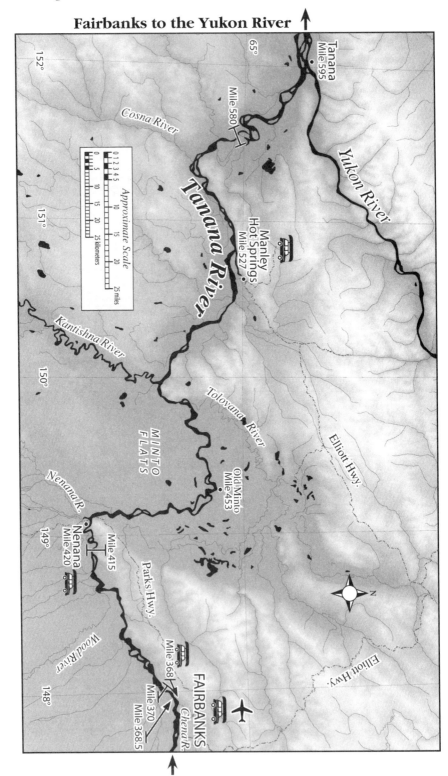

Significant Points

Mile 368.5 (593.3 km): A recreation of a Bush village operated by the River Boat Discovery appears on the left bank as the river turns south from Fairbanks.

Mile 370-385 (595.7-620.0): Houses dot the west hills through here, and, although very few are actually on the river, some are on bluffs and you will be able to hear dogs and road noise. Airboats zip around the swamps to the south and east. You might see a few on the Tanana. But you will definitely hear them. They sound like airplanes perpetually taking off. Airboats are particularly annoying during hunting season, running from the minute after sunrise until the stroke of sunset. There are many moose camps on points through this section; hunters choose their location to see as much river as possible. Be careful about camping in unoccupied spots: some are private camps, so look for No Trespassing signs before making camp.

Fish wheels use the current to turn the baskets, lifting fish from the water, where they slide down to a chute above the axle, which drops them into a pen for collection. Fish wheels, while mechanically much more complicated than nets, can catch much more fish, and are ideally suited for muddy rivers.

Mile 415 (668.2 km): The current slows considerably starting roughly 5 miles before Nenana. It can be a lot of work to fight a headwind through here.

Mile 420 (676.2 km): A grounded paddle boat steamer marks the upriver city limits of Nenana. This is a port town, off-loading freight from the railroad or trucks and loading it onto barges for transport into the roadless Interior. Nenana has all the services of a small town on a highway: two motels, café, small but well-stocked grocery store that even has a good hardware selection—very useful for gear repairs. The city boat launch is by the train depot, a few hundred yards before the Parks Highway bridge. There are a number of landings before this point with varying degrees of public access. Do not leave gear unattended on the beach.

Beyond Nenana, the river leaves the hills behind and winds across the Minto Flats, a fertile wetland with high bird populations. A full day's paddle will roughly cover 20 to 25 miles until the Yukon.

The wide, wide Tanana. When the wind picks up, stick close to shore; there is plenty of fetch for waves to grow.

Mile 453 (729.3 km): Old Minto is now a treatment center closed to the public. Visitors are discouraged. In 1970, the village of Minto moved inland to the Tolovana River to avoid frequent flooding on the Tanana.

Mile 527 (848.5 km): Landing to the town of Manley Hot Springs. If you have a motor or strong arms, you can turn up Manley Hot Springs Slough to get closer to town; otherwise it is a couple of miles walk down the road from the Tanana landing.

Manley sits at the end of the gravel Elliott Highway and is geared to visitors: there is a historic roadhouse with rooms for rent, café, bar, and, last but not least, the hotsprings themselves. They heat a greenhouse and are available by appointment. As a bonus, you can gaze on tropical fruit growing in the subarctic while you soak.

Mile 580-591 (933.8-951.5 km): Barges frequently ground on the shifting mud bars from here through the mouth of the Yukon. Small boats will find plenty of water. But it can get windy, and with a 2 mile wide channel at the mouth, waves can be a serious concern. If it is too windy to paddle, you will have to camp and wait out the weather.

Mile 595 (958.0 km): The village of Tanana—actually on the Yukon—has no road access or regular large cargo plane service. The nearest village with planes capable of flying out a canoe or kayak is Galena, 170 miles down the Yukon. And so, unless you have a folding boat, turn to the Yukon River section of this guidebook.
Ta da!

Porcupine River

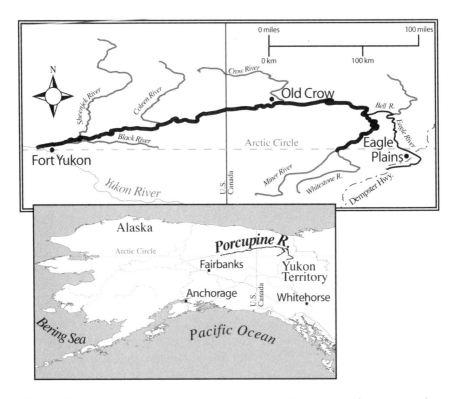

The Porcupine River is the second largest tributary to the Yukon River. The 517 miles of channel flow almost entirely above the Arctic Circle through the wintering grounds of the famous Porcupine caribou herd (though they are not along the banks in summer). With just one village in the middle of the Porcupine, Old Crow, and one at the mouth, Fort Yukon, this is the least populated major drainage in Alaska or the Yukon Territory.

The Ramparts of the Porcupine, rising from the flats below Old Crow, mark the start of over 100 miles of canyon. This is sublime paddling. The swirling sandstone and basalt walls make for lovely gazing while you drift with the pleasant current. Game trails are so numerous, the hills look like an overgrazed pasture. The human touch is almost nonexistent here. There are several ghost towns in the canyons and a few abandoned fish camps, but that is it.

The Ramparts spill into the sinuous Porcupine Flats. This sluggish stretch of river meanders through sloughs and lakes for another 100 miles. The wind frequently blows upriver during the day and it is necessary to paddle through the calm, bright night. This is a rare opportunity to see active nocturnal animals, such as a wolverine waddling along shore, or a wolf pack hunting. The fertile country also attracts birds and other wildlife, and the sandhill crane viewing is guaranteed excellent.

The upper Porcupine River is a little less spectacular than these lower sections, but is not without highlights. The tight winding approach along Eagle River is frequently filled with large male moose, sometimes creating too much excitement. Paddlers will almost certainly spot some wildlife in Salmon Cache Canyon—for whatever reason, wolves like to hunt the upriver part of a canyon, while brown bears work the lower part. When you come to the village of Old Crow, you will find people there used to and accepting of paddlers.

Planning the Paddle

Where does the Porcupine begin and end?

Geographically, the beginning of the Porcupine is straightforward: the Miner and Whitestone Rivers join to make the Porcupine. But very few paddlers begin at this point since you must fly in with a small plane and land on a gravel bar in the river—in other words, starting here is tricky, expensive, and limits you to a folding boat. Instead, most paddlers approach the Porcupine River from Eagle River, which is really a large creek crossed by the gravel Dempster Highway. The Eagle eventually flows into the Bell River, which quickly joins the Porcupine a little below its geographic start.

Another popular approach to the Porcupine begins from a float-plane on Bell Lake, the source for the Bell River, and follows that stream down to the Porcupine. This is more scenic, faster, and easier paddling than following Eagle River, but also has the disadvantage of being expensive and limited to folding boats. Therefore, it is not covered in this book.

Another popular option is to skip the upper river entirely. Old Crow has regular cargo and passenger plane service out of Dawson and Whitehorse. This concentrates the trip on the Ramparts and the Flats, which many people find to be the most exciting stretch of water.

The Porcupine is so remote there are only a few options for shorter trips. Old Crow is the only spot to pull out midriver. Fort Yukon sits at the end of the Porcupine, the Yukon River junction. Its airport is the hub for northern Interior villages in Alaska and there is regularly scheduled cargo and passenger plane service. Another option is to paddle another three to six days through the Yukon Flats to pull out at Yukon Crossing, which has cheap van service for people and boats to Fairbanks.

Paddling Skills

The Porcupine River is almost entirely Class I flat water, with some Class II riffles through the Ramparts of the Porcupine. But the canyons funnel wind, and the water here can turn rough—you must pull over and wait out the weather when this happens.

The Flats are slow to stagnant; when the wind blows upriver—and it frequently does—you will have to camp during the day and paddle at night to make decent progress without wearing yourself out. Paddling through the twilight at three in the morning is a gorgeous and rare experience.

Although the water is mostly flat and easy to paddle, you must be an experienced wilderness traveler on this river—Old Crow is the only place to pull out. If you get in trouble, do not expect another person to come along for at least a week.

Halfway Rock watches over the Ramparts of the Porcupine.

Timing

The Porcupine can be floated from June to September. All other things being equal, higher water is better than lower water since so much of the river is sluggish. June and July can be warm, and will certainly be buggy. August is usually wet and cold, and in September hunters travel the river in skiffs and bears are much more active along the riverbank

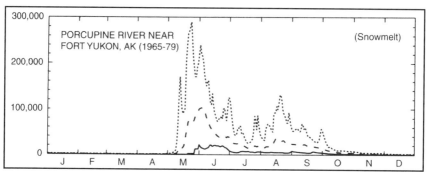

Reproduced with permission from Brabets, Timothy P. and others, Environmental and Hydrologic Overview of the Yukon River Basin, Alaska and Canada. *Water Resources Investigations Report 99-4202, US Geological Survey, Anchorage, AK, 2000.*

than at other times of year. Allow at least a month to go from Eagle River to Yukon Crossing, three weeks for Eagle River to Fort Yukon, 10 to 12 days for Eagle River to Old Crow, and roughly 14 days for the segment from Old Crow to Fort Yukon.

Boat Type

The Porcupine is not terribly windy or choppy, so the choice between a canoe or a sea kayak depends only on how much food you want to carry and which boat type you like better and are the most familiar with. Rafts are useless in the sluggish current. Folding boats do rather well since the shore is frequently muddy and you will rarely drag bottom in the wide, deep channels.

Weather and Water

This trip is above the Arctic Circle. While the air is mostly dry continental air and can be surprisingly warm, the weather—even in July—can be downright terrible. Even if it is 80 degrees, that does not mean a few days later snow and rain won't be driven into your face by 40 mile-an-hour winds. You have to be ready for the full spectrum of conditions from heat exhaustion, to wet, windy, and hovering around freezing.

Drinking Water

Water is a bit of a problem on the Porcupine—particularly along Eagle River, which drains sloughs almost its entire length. This swamp water is a dull to bright red from suspended iron—decaying vegetation turns the water acid, corroding bedrock, and suspending the metal in solution. This staining is difficult if not impossible to get out by straining, boiling, or any other means. It will not cause health problems beyond a touch of the trots as your body adjusts. You just have to deal with it. Below Eagle River, the staining decreases, but the Porcupine never entirely gets rid of the iron. There are more clear feeders into the main stem below the Bell River mouth, so if you are worried about iron, bring large jugs to load up when you do find clear water.

Gear

Getting a boat to the headwaters and then getting it back home is the trickiest bit. Do not expect to sell your boat in Old Crow—they get a quite a few paddlers coming through. Large cargo planes service Old Crow regularly and rates out of the village are relatively reasonable. Fort Yukon has large freight planes, too. You can also paddle across the Yukon Flats to take out with a vehicle or by public van service.

International Concerns

The Porcupine flows through Canada and the United States. There is a RCMP and Canada Customs post at Old Crow. It is not necessary to stop here if you already have checked in at the border when you originally crossed into Canada. There is no U.S. Customs check-in at Fort Yukon or at any other point downriver from the Porcupine on the Yukon.

Maps

The Canadian 1:250,000 maps are:
    Eagle River
    Bell River
    Old Crow
The USGS 1:250,000 maps are:
    Colleen
    Black River
    Fort Yukon

Rest and Resupply Points

River Mile/km	Town & Zip Code	Road	Cargo Plane	Grocery Store	Café
0	Dempster Highway Crossing•	✓			✓
241/388	Old Crow, YT Y0B1N0		✓		✓
515/829.3	Fort Yukon, AK 99740		✓		✓

•No Post Office

Porcupine River Guide

Eagle River to Old Crow

Miles: 241 miles/388 km

Estimated Time: 12 to 15 days

Water Class/Hazards: Class I

Access: At kilometerpost 373 on the Dempster Highway, there is an unimproved access to the Eagle River. Do not park your vehicle here unattended. Instead, make arrangements with the Eagle Plains truck stop for parking.

Maps: Natural Resources Canada 1:250,000 maps:
Eagle River
Bell River
Old Crow

Rest and Restocking: Arrive with all food and gear needed for the journey. Eagle Plains has a motel, gas station, shop, café, and convenience store for small items.

Eagle Plains Hotel
Bag Service 2735
Whitehorse, YT Y1A 3V5
(867)993-2453

Old Crow has a full range of Bush village services, including bed and breakfasts.

Weather: Continental weather.

Section Description

Eagle River quickly leaves the Dempster Highway behind. The creek makes many tight bends as it smoothly and gently flows through low hills and extensive sloughs. The farther you get from the highway, the more the current slows and the muddier the banks get. A couple days into the float it will become harder and harder to find a camp spot with firm footing. In wet years, the bugs can be almost nightmarish on this small, wind-sheltered river. In 4,000 miles of paddling in Alaska and the Yukon, this is the only stretch of water where I have ever had to wear a headnet while paddling. The moose are driven nearly insane by the bugs, too. Expect to see at least a few large, slightly aggressive bulls standing in the water, trying to escape the bites. Give them plenty of space and let them move on at their own pace. The upside to the bugs is the bird life. Expect to see plenty of fuzzy geese chicks and their protective parents. It is difficult to determine precise location visually on the Eagle River since there are so few obvious landmarks, but expect this stretch to take four to five days. It is possible to estimate your position by familiarity with your pace. GPS receivers work, too.

The Bell River is a little wider, faster, and has much colder water than Eagle River. It passes quickly

The Porcupine is wide and slow. The stretch between the Bell River mouth and Old Crow is prime wintering ground for the famous Porcupine caribou herd, but they will not be here in summer. The canyons and hills will be a welcome change of scenery. The river is now marked by long, slow, straight stretches, where you watch the evening's destination for hours before you reach it. Riffles with faster water punctuate the flat water. The associated gravel bars make excellent camps.

Eagle River Crossing to Salmon Cache Canyon

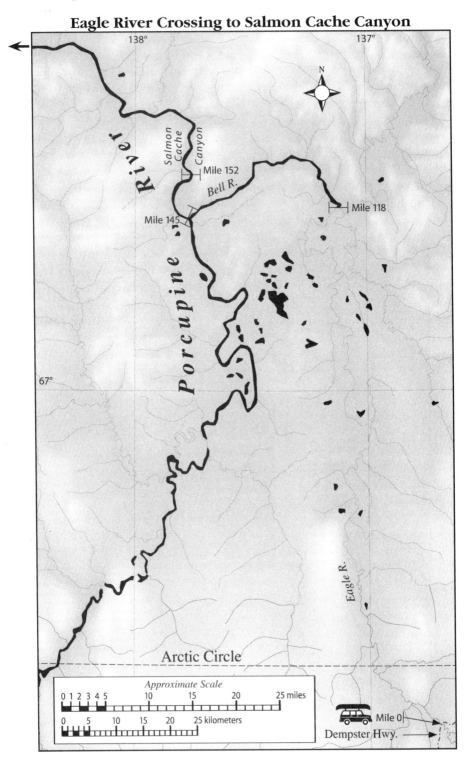

Salmon Cache Canyon to Old Crow ↑

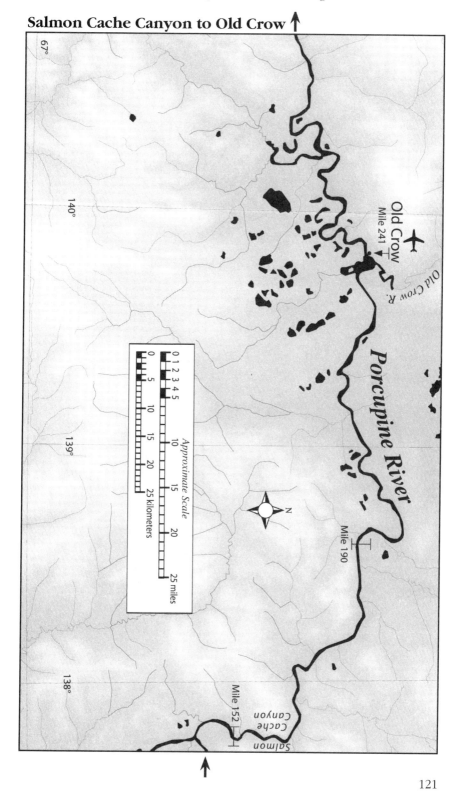

Significant Points

Mile 0: The unimproved put-in at Eagle River bridge on the Dempster Highway. Follow Eagle River for 118 miles to the Bell River. There are many tight, winding sections of this slow creek, so allow four to five days to make it to the Bell. Campsites become increasingly muddy. If you find reasonably firm ground within a half hour of quitting for the day, you will probably want to stop then since you are unlikely to find firmer ground any time soon.

Mile 118 (190 km): The Bell is faster, clearer, and colder than Eagle River, and probably a welcome sight—it will be the first decent landmark to let you know where you are in a few days.

Mile 145 (233.5 km): The Porcupine River! It's wide and muddy.

Mile 152 (244.8 km): The first firm shore is Salmon Cache Canyon. Watch for lots of critters strolling the beach, including wolves and brown bears. Don't camp near the mouths of tributary creeks.

Eagle River is a narrow, winding approach to the Porcupine River. It is optimistically named; Eagle Creek is more accurate. The channel is narrow, a little sluggish, and the banks are muddy.

Mile 190 (305.9 km): At roughly this landmarkless point, there is a newly constructed RCMP cabin on the north bank. It is unmarked on the NRCanada map, but has flagpoles in front of it and is unmissable. The cabin is intermittently staffed by RCMP officers from Old Crow.

Mile 190-240 (305.9-386.5 km): The river from here to Old Crow has long, straight stretches that pass slowly. Just keep repeating to yourself, "Just because you can see it, doesn't mean you're there yet," and be patient about arriving at your destination. The flat water is briefly interrupted by gravely riffles. Besides a nice change of pace, these places also make great camp sites.

Mile 241 (388 km): Old Crow. You will first see the bizarre tent that

Old Crow is the only village on the Porcupine. The large tent covers the hockey rink is winter; it will be the first thing you see on the approach to the village.

shelters the hockey rink in winter. Then, the old downtown appears on a steep cutbank. Just past here the beach widens, flattens out, and makes for nice camping. The services are in the older part of town and parallel the river—grocery store, café, and so forth. If you have trouble finding your way around, just ask; people are used to paddlers and generally friendly.

Old Crow was only settled fully in the 1920s. Many Natives here are related to people in Fort Yukon, with cousins residing in the separate communities. The United States and Canada border now separates the two groups. If you paddle past Old Crow, you will pass Old Crow's precursor communities: Rampart House, Old Rampart, and Fort Yukon (now a large village), the old Hudson Bay trading posts where the mostly migrant Natives traded with outsiders. The posts were continually pushed east in boundary disputes with the United States, finally settling at Old Crow to be near the Porcupine caribou herd wintering ground and the fur-rich swamps of Old Crow Flats.

There are many well constructed older buildings lining the river. This Anglican church is one of the best examples.

Old Crow is a paddler's delight. A gently sloping gravel beach provides many peaceful, firm camp spots. Gasoline is flown in, and therefore expensive; the constant chainsaw buzz of four-wheelers that usually fills Bush villages is only a gentle background hum here. There is a very well stocked store, post office, showers, RCMP post, and small café. A couple of bed and breakfasts line the riverbank. The public phone outside the RCMP post is frequently broken, but there is a reliable one in the arctic entry to the tribal office. There is even a hockey rink, although it is only usable in winter. This is a dry community and you should not bring in alcohol.

Porcupine River Guide

Old Crow to Fort Yukon

Miles: 276 miles/444.4 km

Water Class/Hazards: I-II. The riffly sections can be whipped into rough water by wind or high water.

Estimated Time: 14 to 17 days

Access: Fly into Old Crow
  Air North
  Passenger Reservations and/or cargo:
  USA (800) 764-0407
  Canada (800) 661-0407
  www.flyairnorth.com

Outfitters: None

Rest and Restocking: Old Crow and Fort Yukon have a full range of services

Maps: Natural Resources Canada 1:250,000:
  Old Crow

  USGS 1:250,000:
  Colleen
  Black River
  Fort Yukon

Section Description

There are two distinct parts of this stretch: the Ramparts and the Flats. The Ramparts last for over 100 miles, and are gorgeous cliffs that guide the river. The Flats are slow, winding sloughs full of wildlife: sandhill cranes, scads of moose, and, in the clear tributaries, pike, grayling, and sheefish fishing so good, all you need is a hook to catch fish.

Old Crow to the Coleen River

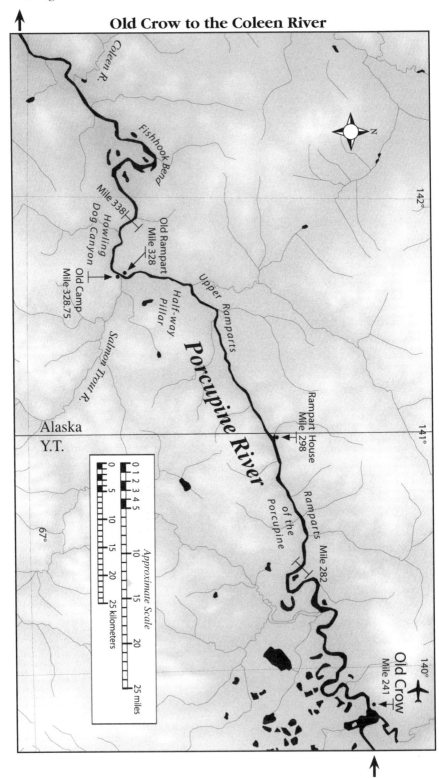

Coleen River to Fort Yukon

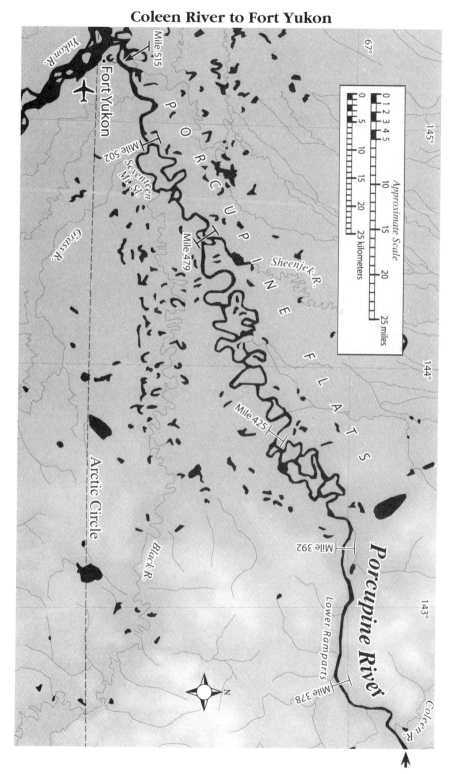

Significant Points

Mile 282 (454 km): The Ramparts of the Porcupine are reason enough to do this trip. The water picks up speed even through the flat parts, and even gets a little riffly through the odd gravel patch. The cliffs are gorgeous. Swirls of basalt, sandstone, and limestone confine the river, and you can stare off into the hills and daydream. The gaps in

The Ramparts of the Porcupine are some of the loveliest paddling anywhere.

The Rampart House in 2002. The abandoned village is undergoing restoration by carpenters from Old Crow and will probably have changed since this picture was taken. It is rare to find an entire town in this excellent state of preservation. The only way to reach it is by boat.

the rock are laced with game trails so thick they look like a pasture. Watch for brown bears and wolves on shore.

Mile 298 (480 km): Rampart House. This ghost town was originally a Hudson Bay fur trading post directly on the border between the United States and Canada. Abandoned just before World War I in favor of Old Crow, the post was operated into the 1930s by independent fur traders. The village is in the process of being restored by carpenters from Old Crow.

Mile 328 (528.2 km): Old Rampart is almost impossible to find, but it really is there in the brush. Stick right next to shore, looking for a faint path. There are a few cabins behind the willows—it is nowhere near as spectacular as Rampart House—and lots and lots of mosquitoes.

Mile 328.75 (529.4 km): Lots of mosquitoes guard the private property at Old Camp at the mouth of the Salmon Trout River. This tributary is as clear as air. If there is enough of a breeze to hold down the bugs, the fishing can be phenomenal.

Mile 338 (544.3 km): Howling Dog Rock marks the pause between the Upper and Lower Ramparts. It acquired its name when the dogs that used to pull boats upriver reached this point, ran out of shore, had to jump in and swim, and began their howling protests.

Mile 378 (608.7 km): The Lower Ramparts begin. The current is never as fast nor are the walls nearly as dramatic through this shorter section of Ramparts. Burnt Paw and John Herbert's Village no longer have buildings.

These rocky bluffs mark the last of the Ramparts and the beginning of the winding sloughs.

Mile 392 (631.2 km): The Porcupine Flats begin. The current slows to a crawl. The channel, islands, and sloughs at the entrance to the Flats are changed in detail since the USGS map was made and will look considerably different depending on the water level. It is impossible to get lost; just relax, stop paddling for a bit, and let the boat drift to find the fastest current to help choose which channel to follow. If it says, "slough" on the map, don't go there unless you want to earn every inch of forward progress while getting eaten alive by mosquitoes.

Mile 425 (684.4 km): There are very few islands below where Joe Ward Camp used to be, but the gravely bends make for dry, relatively bug free-spots. The water can be swimmably warm all through the Flats.

Mile 479 (771.3 km): The mouth of the Sheenjek River has great grayling fishing. Many villagers motor up from Fort Yukon to fish here.

Mile 502 (808.4 km): The mouth of the Black River and the associated Seventeen Mile Slough are popular swimming and water-skiing spots for Fort Yukoners.

Mile 515 (829.3 km): Finding the slough to Fort Yukon is tricky. Stick tightly to the left bank as you float past Homebrew Island. It will be confusing picking which island is Homebrew out of all the other unmapped sloughs, islands, and gravel bars on the approach. This is one of the few times a GPS is handy on a river. A very faint four-wheeler trail on shore is the only indication you have found the right channel. Turn into this mouth and paddle 2 or 3 miles upriver against fairly stagnant water to get to the beach by the airport.

If faster, gray water starts mixing with the Porcupine brown, you passed the turnoff and are starting to join the Yukon. If you absolutely have to reach Fort Yukon, turn around now and paddle upriver to try and find the entrance. It will be much easier paddling against the Porcupine than a two-mile struggle against the powerful Yukon to reach the beach.

Fort Yukon is a large, full-service community. There are daily cargo and passenger planes to Fairbanks and on to Anchorage, as well as bed and breakfasts, grocery store, washeteria, and café. Fort Yukon is a wet village, whose airport serves as a transportation hub to surrounding dry villages. Many people come to Fort Yukon just to drink. Camping on the beach is not recommended and if you plan to spend the night you should either have friends in the village or stay at a bed and breakfast.

Many paddlers continue through the Yukon Flats and take out at the Dalton Highway crossing. That section of river is covered in the Yukon section of this book.

Ta da!

Koyukuk River

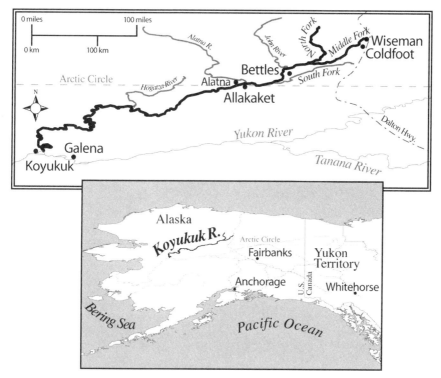

The Koyukuk River is one of the least-paddled rivers in this guidebook. This is partially because it is difficult to get to and leave. But the prospect of a slow, winding slog through the swamps in the lower half of the river further discourages even the most determined paddlers. Because of these drawbacks, the third-longest river in the Yukon drainage crosses some of the most remote, fertile, and wildlife-rich country in the world.

Below Bettles, there are very few paddlers. Below the twin villages of Allakaket and Alatna at the Arctic Circle, there are even less—locals say a paddler wanders down the river every two or three years. There is also very little skiff traffic; expect to see another boat only every three to six days. This lack of humans, combined with the vicious mosquitoes in the forests, means the banks of the Koyukuk provides awesome summer wildlife viewing from the river. On rarely traveled stretches, moose lie on almost every river bend chewing their cud, bears stroll the shore, and even wolf packs sleep in the open. Sandhill cranes nest so thickly the squawking of the startled birds will constantly echo up and down the silent channel.

The Koyukuk River was only sparsely inhabited by Natives when miners, disappointed to discover all the good claims above Dawson taken, traveled farther down the Yukon and then up the Koyukuk in search of good digging. They finally found it all the way upstream at Coldfoot—named because shortly after the miners founded the city, everyone hustled out of the area in shock as winter descended.

Koyukuk River Guide

Planning the Paddle

Where does the Koyukuk begin and end?

There are three upper forks of the Koyukuk—the North, Middle, and South. The North Fork flows through the Gates of the Arctic National Park and is the most heavily paddled stretch of the drainage—the village of new Bettles' primary industry is flying visitors into this country. The Middle Fork is less heavily traveled but is accessible from the Dalton Highway. Its channel parallels the road and the trans-Alaska pipeline for more than 40 river miles. The South Fork should not be paddled since it is choked with sweepers well below the highway crossing.

Just a lonely canoe, stunted spruce trees, and a thin strip of water above the Arctic Circle.

The Koyukuk River enters the Yukon through a series of sloughs. The village of Koyukuk sits right at the junction. Downstream, the nearest village capable of flying out a hard-shell boat is St. Marys, a roughly 400-mile float on the Yukon. The village of Emmonak is 80 miles further down the Yukon from St. Marys, and most paddlers will probably want to continue on to there, since that is the practical end of the Yukon. Just 30 miles up the Yukon from the village of Koyukuk is the village of Galena. It is almost impossible to paddle against the current and there is no regular public transportation between the two villages capable of carrying a hard-shell boat—although there are regular mail planes between Koyukuk and Galena capable of carrying folding boats. Skiff drivers have given rides to paddlers and their boats from Koyukuk to Galena for a reasonable price, but don't count on it. The best way to pull out with a hard-shell is to follow the Yukon downriver, or bring a folding boat and fly out from Koyukuk or any other village.

Paddling Skills

There are only a few Class II riffles on the Koyukuk forks, but the North and Middle Forks are more difficult to paddle than their class rating implies. These feeders are braided glacial outflow streams and the main channel can be tricky to find and follow. They are not the toughest braided sections to paddle in this book, but this is not the place to learn to paddle braided water. The Forks are rarely traveled, and if you get into trouble, you will be on your own.

The main stem Koyukuk River is completely flat water. And below Hughes, the current is somewhere between sluggish and a lake. You have to be a strong, steady paddler and should count on taking more rest days than usual to maintain the exertion of earning all forward progress. It is useless to fight any sort of headwind through here, so, you either have to paddle at night when it's still, or wait out wind you could paddle through on most other rivers.

Timing

As the USGS chart shows, the Koyukuk has dramatically higher

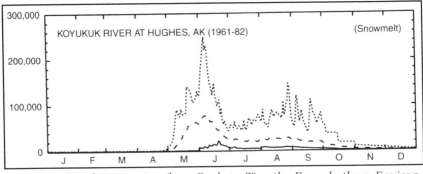

Reproduced with permission from Brabets, Timothy P. and others, Environmental and Hydrologic Overview of the Yukon River Basin, Alaska and Canada. *Water Resources Investigations Report 99-4202, US Geological Survey, Anchorage, AK, 2000.*

flows in late May and early June, before drying to a relative trickle for the rest of the summer. This is because the basin is almost entirely permafrost. As the snow melts, it rushes into the channel without soaking into the ground for slow release over the summer, and the water level is strongly seasonal. When paddling the whole river, the best time to set out is early to mid-June. This early start allows enough time for the any ice still in the channel to work itself out, but the water is still high enough for easy paddling. This also means you are paddling the big Yukon during early summer when the weather and water are relatively mild.

This is not to say that leaving later in the year is impossible; it will just be more work. The lower river from Hughes to the Yukon is all but stagnant then. Additionally, the heavily braided forks are much shallower late in summer, so you will have to hop out of the boat and drag it over gravel beds more frequently than usual through this stretch. If you are starting in July, it can be a good idea to put in downstream at Coldfoot rather than Wiseman since the river through here is very shallow at this time of year.

Boat Type

Hard-shell kayaks or canoes work equally well on this narrow river—wind is not much of a concern, nor are waves. On the upper forks, a small, easily maneuverable boat is nice to make quick turns around the gravel bars, but a larger boat will still work fine.

Folding boats are unusually well suited to the Koyukuk since they are easy to fly out in even the smallest mail plane. Wind is not much of a problem on the relatively narrow channel, so the lack of a keel is not the usual hassle. The cloth skin can be a slight, but not insurmountable difficulty on the upper forks as you grind over the inevitable gravel bar. The only drawbacks with folding boats on the Koyukuk are the standard ones: small carrying capacity and the need to unload them nightly and stake them near the tent to listen for porcupines gnawing on the wooden frames.

Food-carrying capacity of the boat is a general concern. There are no large grocery stores in any of the small villages of the Koyukuk, so if you are unable to resupply by mailing food packages, you must have enough free space in the boat to carry food to last the entire trip.

Weather and Water

The river is generally ice free and flowing the entire distance by late May or early June. Ice can dam the mouth of the Koyukuk after cold, snowy winters, and cause flooding at the mouth. Waiting until early or middle June will eliminate this potential hazard.

Although half of the river is above the Arctic Circle, from June until the middle of August, most years it is relatively dry, sunny, and warm. Thunderstorms can quickly erupt in the afternoons, spitting cold rain, lightning, and thunder. The raindrops are frigid, but most rainsqualls are short, and it should be easy to keep your gear warm and dry. The lightning causes frequent forest fires in the peat hills along the upper river valley, and wood smoke will rise from the almost perpetual smoldering. You should be safe from almost all forest fires on the river.

Occasionally, it can rain every day for a month, pour inches of rain in a day, or even snow. Although these are exceptions, you should be prepared to handle this full spectrum of conditions.

Drinking Water

The river is moderately muddy and silty above Bettles, and although boiling and settling overnight is the most reliable way to make drinking water, at most water levels it is probably even possible to pump through a standard water filter without clogging it too frequently.

This starts to change roughly below the Arctic Circle; the current slows considerably and is fed from swamps. The water from these swamps has a fairly high iron content due to the natural acidity of standing water. It shouldn't cause any health problems and you can ignore the light red stain. If you can't ignore the color, there are many clear feeders that are easy to paddle to, so you might want to bring jugs large enough to gather the water before camping at night.

Gear

The biggest material obstacle to floating the Koyukuk, is, as usual, the boat. There is bus service from Fairbanks to Coldfoot and Wiseman to put in on the Middle Fork. The Upper Fork is accessible only by small planes based out of either Fairbanks or Bettles. Getting out is the trick. You can leave from any village on the river with a folding boat; if you have a hard-shell, you will have to paddle the Yukon at least as far as St. Marys, if not to the delta, unless you can figure a way up the 30 miles to Galena.

Be sure to have bomb-proof bug protection. Mosquitoes can be bad through here, even by Alaska standards. Have an excellent repair kit for tent zippers and mesh patches. If bugs can get at you at night, you will not be able to sleep.

Maps

The USGS 1:250,000 maps are:
Wiseman
Bettles
Hughes
Melozitna
Kateel River
Shungnak
Nulato

Rest and Resupply Points

Fairbanks, 260 miles south of Coldfoot, is the nearest large city and the best place to load up on groceries before traveling the Koyukuk.

All villages in this remote section of the Interior are quite small, and the correspondingly small stores make it difficult, but not impossible, to stock up.

Bettles is the largest, best-supplied village on this trip. During freeze-up in the winter it is possible to drive from Bettles to the Haul Road on a cat trail, so prices and food selection are decent by Bush standards. The store is about as well stocked as a big-city convenience store. There is also a café and the lodge operates a bunkhouse. All the other villages are rarely visited, do not have formal accommodations for people from out of town, and have a very limited selection and volume of food. Alakaket/Alatna, Hughes, and Huslia are dry villages, and possession of alcohol is illegal.

River Mile/km	Town & Zip Code	Road	Cargo Plane	Grocery Store	Café
0	Wiseman No PO	✓			
15/24.2	Coldfoot 9970	✓			✓
75/120.8	Bettles 99726				✓
153/246.3	Allakaket 99720				
225/362.3	Hughes 99745				
392/631.1	Huslia 99746				
585/941.9	Koyukuk 99754				

Koyukuk River Guide

North Fork of the Koyukuk

Miles: 80 miles to the Middle Fork, and a further 22 miles to Bettles

Estimated Time: 3 to 5 days

Water Class/Hazards: Class I Squaw Rapids is marked on the map, but is only a noticeable riffle under certain water conditions. There are many heavily braided sections with shallow water, sweepers, and snags to avoid.

Access: Float or wheel planes provide the only access to the North Fork.

Sourdough Outfitters
PO Box 26066
Bettles Field, AK 99726
(907)692-5252
www.sourdoughoutfitters.com

Brooks Range Aviation
PO Box 10
Bettles, AK 99726
(800) 692-5443
www.brooksrange.com

Maps: USGS 1:250,000
 Wiseman
 Bettles

Outfitters: The nearest suppliers are in Fairbanks. Fairbanks is the second-largest city in Alaska and has excellent services from grocery stores to outdoor gear and boat suppliers to plane service.

Rest and Restocking: Bettles has a café, bunkhouse, and store.

Weather: After the snow finally melts in the beginning of June, the weather is remarkably warm and frequently sunny, with the odd cold thunderstorm in the afternoon. There are frequent forest fires in the surrounding hills, but they do not cause problems for river travelers.

Section Description

The North Fork is the most heavily paddled section of the Koyukuk for good reason: it passes through the Gates of the Arctic, past the towering Frigid Crags and Boreal Mountain. This section of river names the Gates of the Arctic National Park, and the entire North Fork falls within the park boundaries and a wilderness subsection of the park. This stretch is also the most expensive to access.

The scenery is mind blowing besides the Gates. Bare, tundra covered hills rise up from either side of the valley. The water is glacial green, the grayling fishing is excellent, and except for some braids, the water is flat and easy to paddle. The tundra is mostly permafrost, which absorbs water poorly. Keep an eye out for rapidly rising river levels and choppier paddling after a heavy rain.

Koyukuk North Fork

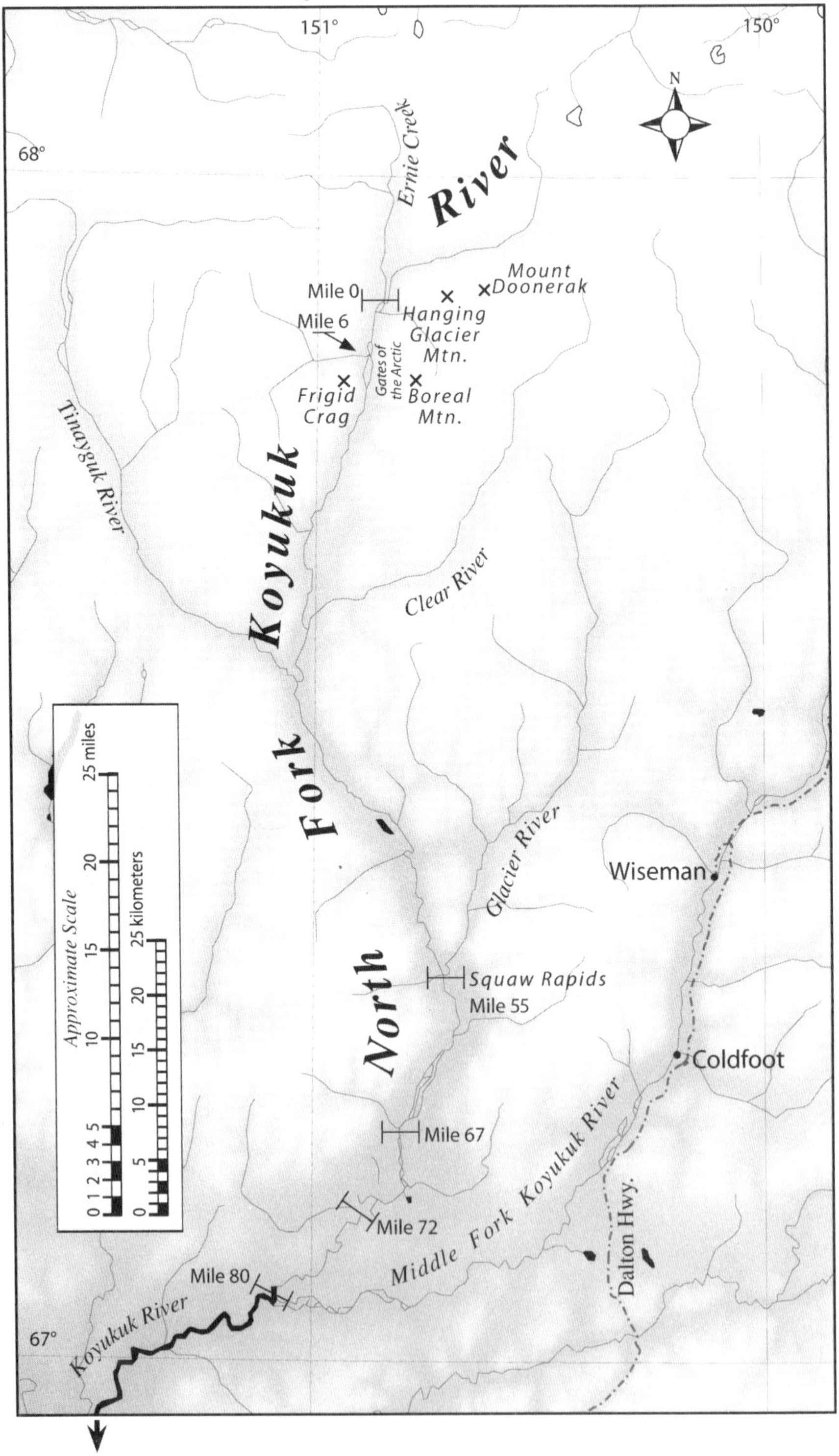

Significant Points

Mile 0: Land anywhere the pilot knows is safe to land. This mileage count begins at the junction with Ernie Creek.

Mile 6 (9.7 km): The Gates of the Arctic. Boreal Mountain and the Frigid Crags tower over each side of the North Fork.

Mile 55 (88.6 km): Squaw Rapids is some small waves and chop below the Glacier River mouth. If you get low in the boat and treat the obstacle with respect, it will not be a difficult run.

Mile 67 (107.9 km): The river slows, splits, and enters an open swamp.

Mile 72 (115.9 km): Back to a single channel.

Mile 80 (128.8 km): Join the Middle Fork to make the official Koyukuk River. Jump ahead in this guide to Mile 53 of the Middle Fork section.

Savor the steady current of the upper river. It slows considerably below Allakaket and Alatna.

The Middle Fork and the
Koyukuk to Allakaket/Alatna/

Miles: Coldfoot to new Bettles is 60 miles (96.6 km). Add 15 miles (26.2 km) if starting from Wiseman.

Estimated Time: Roughly 3 days to Bettles, 5 to 7 days from Coldfoot to Allakaket/Alatna

Water Class/Hazards: All of the Middle Fork is technically Class I flatwater. However, the upper river consists of braided gravel bars until below Windy Arm. The main Koyukuk River is flat water and not much disturbed by wind.

Access: The Dalton Highway parallels the Middle Fork from Coldfoot to Wiseman.

Sourdough Outfitters
PO Box 26066
Bettles Field, AK 99726
(907)692-5252
www.sourdoughoutfitters.com

Brooks Range Aviation
PO Box 10
Bettles, AK 99726
(800) 692-5443
www.brooksrange.com

Dalton Highway Express provides van service from Fairbanks up the Dalton Highway to Coldfoot or Wiseman for people, hard-shell boats, and gear—boats and gear are an additional, reasonable charge. They can drop you off almost at the river's edge. Call them beforehand to make reservations and be sure to mention you are bringing a boat, since not all the vans have racks.

Dalton Highway Express
(907) 474-3555
www.daltonhighwayexpress.com

Maps: USGS 1:250,000:
  Wiseman
  Bettles

Outfitters: The nearest suppliers are in Fairbanks. Fairbanks is the second-largest city in Alaska and has excellent services from grocery stores to outdoor gear and boat suppliers to plane service.

Rest and Restocking: Wiseman is a tiny, active mining community, established in 1908. Many buildings are historic cabins. There is a post office, small store, bed & breakfast, and small, but excellent, museum.

Coldfoot, just like the t-shirt says, is the farthest-north truck stop in the United States. There is a café, motel, showers, post office, and airstrip, but no real grocery store.

Bettles has a café, bunkhouse, store, and guide service.

Weather: After the snow finally melts in the beginning of June, the weather is remarkably warm and frequently sunny, with the odd cold thunderstorm in the afternoon. There are frequent forest fires in the surrounding hills, but they do not cause problems for river travelers.

Section Description

The Middle Fork of the Koyukuk is a delightful paddle. The streambed is braided gravel, and the water is a spectacular shade of glacial green. The Middle Fork is accessible from the Dalton highway, and a van service can drive you and your hard-shell boat from Fairbanks, making this the cheapest, most flexible way to put in on the upper Koyukuk. Although the water is mostly Class I, the braids and small channels make the river a little trickier than the class designation suggests. It helps to be very good at reading currents to pick the main channel. But, as on all braided channels, campsites are numerous, firm, and right next to the water.

Koyukuk Middle Fork

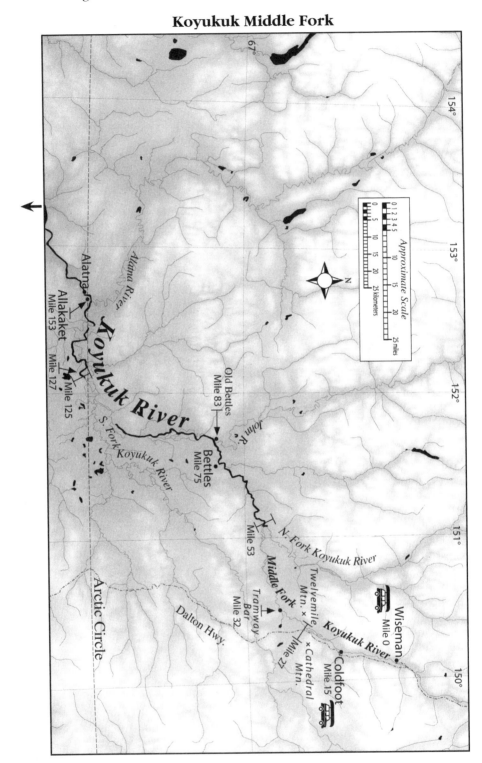

Significant Points

Mile 0: The Middle Fork can get a little low and difficult to float in dry periods. However, early in the summer and during wet periods, Wiseman is an excellent place to put in. The river flows directly against the gravel spur road.

Mile 15 (24.2 km): You can literally drive right to the river. Turn west off the highway at Coldfoot, following the road to the end of the airstrip. From here a series of informal dirt tracks leads to the gravel bars of the river. At lower water, they should be dry enough for a four-wheel drive vehicle, although you might want to walk across the terrain before driving it, just to be sure.

Paddling Braided Rivers

As you paddle a braided river, try to pick the widest channel that holds to the middle of the river. It is always best to paddle with bare gravel bars on both banks. However, if given a choice between a channel lined with cottonwoods or one lined with black spruce, follow the cottonwood channel; eroding banks undercut black spruces, leaving them leaning across the water as sweepers. Cottonwoods and poplars have a much weaker root system and are more likely to wash away from the bank. Also, when you inevitably ground the boat on a shallow gravel bar, hop out on the upstream side. As you push the boat across the rocks, always keep a firm grip on it. And test the water depth before committing your foot to a forward step; the current frequently cuts bars off abruptly.

Mile 27 (43.5 km): After passing between Twelvemile and Cathedral

Mountains, the trans-Alaska pipeline and the odd truck on the Dalton Highway recede behind you, never to reappear.

Mile 32 (51.5 km): A private cabin is at Tramway Bar. There was a roadhouse for a number of decades around in the late 19th century. This site was also one of the earliest gold discoveries on the Koyukuk, with placer gold discovered around 1893.

Mile 53 (85.3 km): The North Fork joins the flow, and the river is now officially the Koyukuk.

Mile 75 (120.8 km): The village of Bettles is called Evansville on the USGS map. The old village of Bettles did not have a suitable location for an airstrip, and by the 1950s most of the community moved to this FAA weather station. A sluggish creek flows into the Koyukuk at the top of the town beach; this can be a good, out-of-the-way spot to park the boat while you wander around town, although it's an unusually buggy spot, too. Town services are all located around the airport. The Park Service and Fish and Wildlife Service maintain visitor's centers. A phone booth at the end of the runway has intermittent 24-hour service (if the phone is working, you can dial from the booth anytime). There is a more mechanically sound public phone in the nearby store and café available during business hours. Sourdough Outfitters operates a bunkhouse and guide service. The 2000 census lists 71 year-round residents for new Bettles, but the summer population is substantially higher as people are brought in from outside to work in the tourism business. Watch for floatplanes landing parallel to the town beach when you leave.

Mile 83 (133.6 km): Old Bettles. Marked "Bettles" on the USGS map, this now abandoned mining town sits just below the mouth of the John River. There are numerous cabins in excellent condition, including—oddly for Alaska—several multistory buildings. There is also lots of old mining equipment: steam boilers, gravel washers, and pumps. It is easy to shoot lots of pictures here. But that is all you should take from the site. Visitors are welcome to wander the streets, but should not disturb anything. Some of these cabins are still used as hunting camps and are privately owned.

Many buildings are on the bluff, overlooking the river. People preferred to live higher in elevation along rivers both to avoid the heavy cold air in winter and to catch summer breezes off the river in summer to keep the bugs down.

The current slows considerably past here.

Old Bettles is now a ghost town. The new Bettles is marked Evans-ville on the USGS map, but every-one calls it Bettles. Just to make things confusing.

Mile 125 (210.3 km): The flash of yellow in the willows on the left bank is a wrecked airplane. The instruments are removed, but trans-portation costs are so high from the Bush that the body of the plane was left behind. I am unable to find in-formation about this crash.

Mile 127 (204.5 km): A large sign on the left bank informs river travelers they are now passing through Native village corporation land (the sign is on a cutbank and could well be washed away by the time this de-

scription is read). The Koyukuk is a navigable river and all land below the high-water line is open to the public. But within the boundaries shown on the sign, it is illegal to trespass above the high-water mark. Outsiders hunt the Koyukuk heavily in the fall and this has been a source of friction over the years. As long as you stay below the high-water mark and respect private property, paddlers are fine.

Mile 153 (246.3 km): Allakaket and Alatna. Hudson Stuck, Archdeacon of the Yukon, founded Allakaket and Alatna. (This was one of many projects undertaken by the ambitious Episcopalian. He also managed to be the first person to climb to the summit of Denali, traveled all over Alaska and the Yukon by dogsled and boat, and wrote several classic books on boreal travel.) His own words describe the founding best: "Back next day at the mouth of the Alatna, I was again impressed with the eligibility of that spot as a mission site. It was but ten miles above the present native village [Moses' Village, now abandoned], and, with church and school established, the whole population would sooner or later move to it. This gives the opportunity for regulating the build-

The tinfoil wallpaper in this Bettles cabin's interior brightens the room during a cold, dark winter.

ing of cabins, and the advantage of a new, clean start. Moreover, the Alatna River is the highway between Kobuk and the Koyukuk, and the Esquimaux coming over in increasing numbers, would be served by a mission at this place as well as the Indians. I foresaw two villages, perhaps, on the opposite sides of the river—one clustered about the church and the school, the other a little lower down—where these ancient hereditary enemies might live side by side in peace and harmony under the firm yet gentle influence of the church. So I staked a mission site, and set up notices claiming ground for that purpose, almost opposite the mouth of the Alatna, which, in the native tongue, is Allakaket or Allachaket" (*10,000 Miles with a Dogsled*, 1914). St. John's-in-the-Wilderness, the log Episcopal church built by Hudson Stuck in 1907, still stands.

The present layout remains true to Stuck's plan: the village of Allakaket sits in the left bank just below the mouth of the Alatna River and just above the Arctic Circle. The village of Alatna is on the right bank, with the landing slightly downriver from Allakaket. Allakaket is mostly Indian and Alatna is mostly Eskimo. Allakaket has the airstrip, and the best place to camp is on the grassy plain, a quick float downriver from the main village landing. There should be a reasonable expectation of privacy here. The water from the Alatna River mouth can surge a couple feet overnight after heavy rains. Set camp high enough to account for unexpected weather both in the village and for roughly 15 miles downriver. You must have a folding boat if you plan to fly out from this community of 170 people.

Allakaket/Alatna to Koyukuk

Distance: 435 miles (700.4 km)

Estimated Time: Allow 14 days at higher water and roughly 21 days at lower water.

Water Class: I—real class one. It's all one sluggish slough.

Access: Access to this section of river is difficult and expensive. You can either paddle a week in from the Dalton Highway, or fly a folding boat in on a mail plane. That is it.

Maps: USGS 1:250,000
  Bettles
  Wiseman
  Hughes
  Melozitna
  Kateel River, Alaska
  Shungnak
  Nulato, Alaska

Outfitters: None

Rest and Restocking: Allakaket/Alatna, Hughes, Huslia, and Koyukuk all have very small grocery stores with a very limited selection—both in terms of quantity and variety of goods. There are no formal visitor facilities in any of these villages.

Weather: Continental

Section Description

This section of the Koyukuk is almost never paddled—it is very hard to get to and get out of, the current is nonexistent, and the banks are a muddy mess. And the mosquitoes are atrocious. It also is home to the most incredible wildlife viewing of any river in this book.

Past Hughes, when the water slows and begins its winding contortions through the swamps, the animals come down to the water's edge in herds. Expect to see wolf packs, black bears, moose on every river bend, and to be accompanied by the eerie warbling of sandhill cranes while paddling the lonely channel. The trick is to think of this section as a lake rather than a river trip; if you don't expect the water to flow, you can relax, take a little pride in your hardening muscles, and enjoy the sights almost no one else gets to see.

You should expect to wake up sharing your camp with moose most mornings between Hughes and Koyukuk. This is either wonderful or a

little scary. Almost all moose will push on if you yell at them in an unthreatening way. Don't push a confrontation. Cows with calves can be particularly touchy; don't get between mom and her baby.

The riverbanks below Hughes and especially below Huslia are very soft sediment that is constantly being reworked and changed by the Koyukuk. The USGS maps were updated in the early to mid-1980s, but expect the river channel to have changed in places since then. The most common change is to have the river cut off what used to be an oxbow and now it flows more directly. There are two instances of this mentioned in the upcoming Significant Points discussion, but the

A wolf pack leaves its tracks in the mud banks on the middle Koyukuk.

channel may change again since this was written. Be prepared to do some original channel reading. If you make a mistake and find yourself in a winding slough, don't worry—you will rejoin the main river eventually. It will just take elbow grease, patience, and time.

Allakaket to Huslia

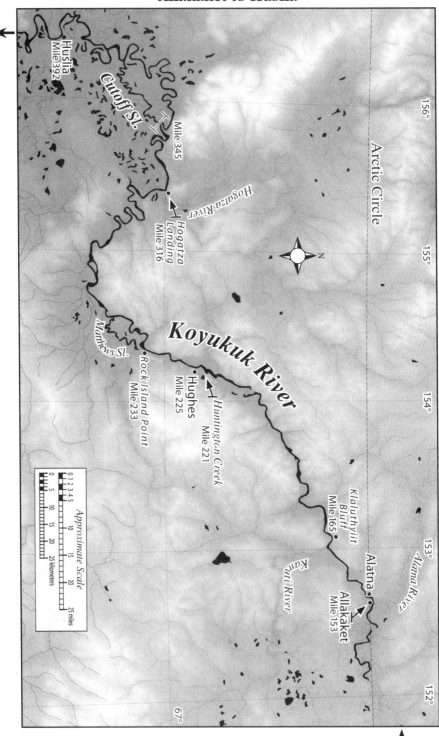

Huslia to Yukon River

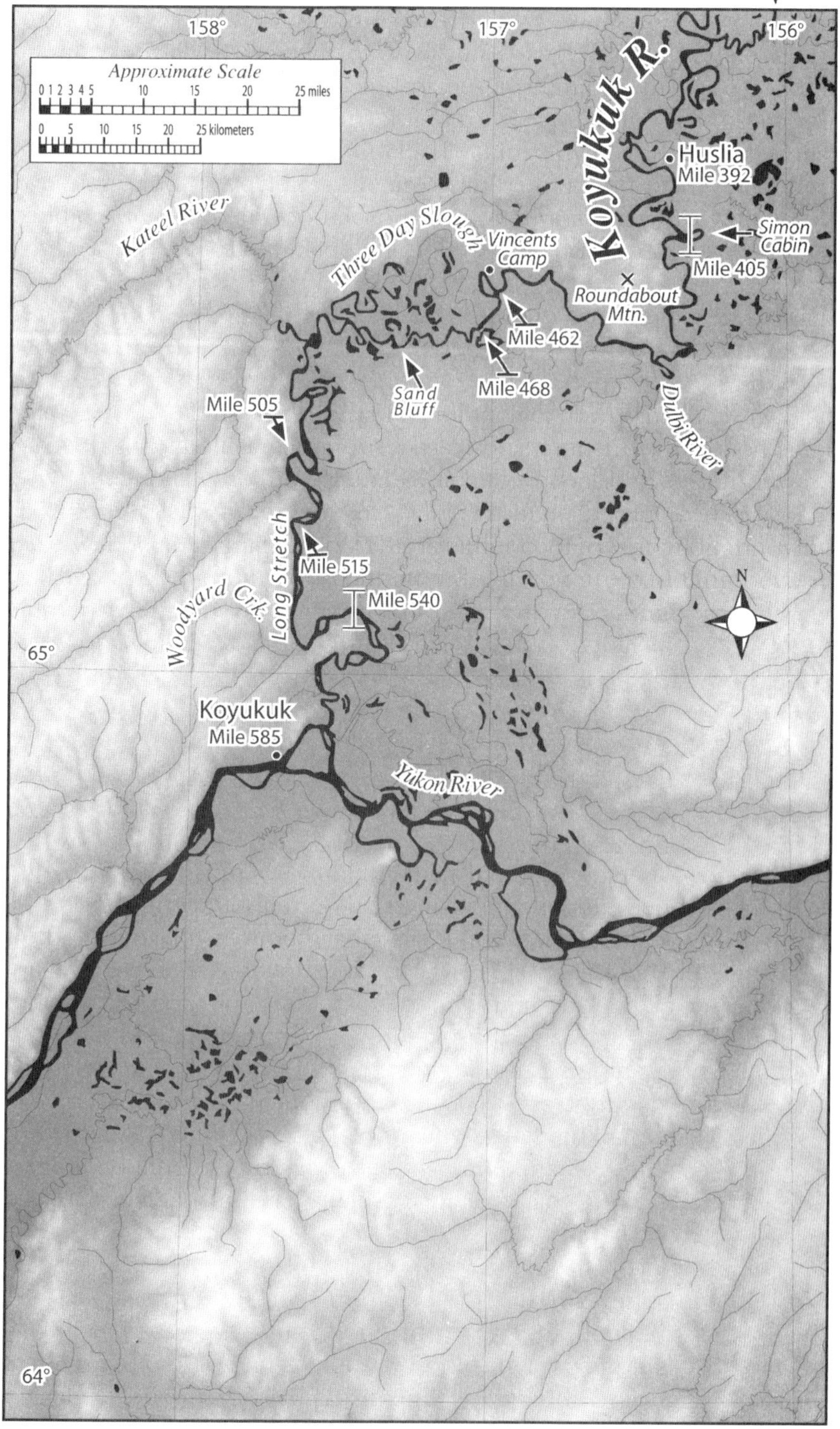

Approximate Scale

0 1 2 3 4 5   10   15   20   25 miles

0   5   10   15   20   25 kilometers

158°

157°

156°

Koyukuk R.

Huslia
Mile 392

Simon Cabin
Mile 405

Kateel River

Three Day Slough

Vincents Camp

× Roundabout Mtn.

Mile 462

Mile 468

Sand Bluff

Mile 505

Dulbi River

Woodyard Crk.

Long Stretch

Mile 515

Mile 540

N

65°

Koyukuk
Mile 585

Yukon River

64°

153

Significant Points

Mile 165 (265.7 km): The water slows again below Klaluthyiit Bluff. A full day's paddle will be 25 to 30 miles.

Mile 221 (355.8 km): The mouth of Huntington Creek, named for the family of James and Sydney Huntington, the respective narrators of *On the Edge of Nowhere* and *Shadows on the Koyukuk*. Reading these books before leaving for the river will expand the experience.

Mile 225 (362.3 km): Hughes is a very small village with only 80 residents on the left bank. It is one of the few Alaska villages to still be mostly log cabins, not premanufactured homes. A small store, post office, and airstrip are the only services here. There is a long, open beach from which it is possible to see the entire village. It was originally founded as a mining camp, but is now a Native village.

Mile 233 (375.1 km): There are some private fish camps on both sides of the river below Rock Island Point. The Koyukuk gets a weak run of king salmon, and if you paddle through around mid-July, you should see orange fillets drying on stick racks and smell alder smoke rising from the smokehouse. The current slows even further past here—expect to work for a 25 mile day through the upcoming bends.

Mile 316 (508.8 km): The mouth of the Hogatza River. A half mile up this river is Hogatza Landing, the terminus of a 30 mile road leading to the Hogatza placer mines. Dredges operated here at least as recently as 1982. As of this writing over twenty years later, none are in operation, nor are there any plans to resume large-scale mining.

Mile 345 (555.5 km): You have a choice: either follow the Cut-off Slough to the left, or go right and follow the main channel. The USGS map is a little deceiving since the river is in the process of changing its path. Cut-off Slough is wider and seems to flow a little faster than the main channel. It has lots of tight little bends but is still probably shorter than the main channel. Combined with the fact that it is the most moose-dense part of a moose-dense river, Cut-off is one slough I recommend following. While traveling this section, it is very difficult to tell where you are since there are no visual landmarks. The slough will be a very full (roughly 10 hours) day's paddle, though.

Mile 392 (631.1 km): Huslia. Set on a steep cutbank, there is very little usable beach at this village of 300 people. Park at the first landing you see for the fastest access to the center of town. There is a post office, airstrip, and small store. Camping on the beach is awkward since there is so little flat space. If you are going to camp, float a little further down to the barge landing.

James Huntington, narrator of *On the Edge of Nowhere*, founded Huslia. His description of this event is not as compact as Hudson Stuck's, so it is not fruitful to quote. To summarize the story: the community that used to live below the mouth of the Hogatza moved here to avoid seasonal flooding and for the unusually good drinking water. In 2001, the casing from the town's first well (now abandoned due to the changing channel) was sticking out from the cutbank.

Mile 405 (652.1 km): The oxbow to Simon Cabin is washed through and stranded. Get used to the view of Roundabout Mountain. You'll be seeing it for a day or two.

The village of Koyukuk has around 100 residents today. Historically, it served as a stop for small steamers before they left the Yukon for the smaller Koyukuk.
(*Jasper Wyman Collection, Anchorage Museum*)

Mile 462 (743.8 km): The oxbow to Vincents Camp is washed through and cut off.

Mile 468 (753.5 km): The island opposite the mouth of Three Day Slough is filled in with sediment and no longer an island.

Mile 505 (813.1 km): The hills on the west shore down to Woodyard Creek are excellent brown bear habitat. Don't set up camp close to feeder streams on this side of the river.

Mile 515 (829.2 km): Long Stretch is just that—a long, straight run to Koyukuk Mountain.

Mile 540 (869.4 km): The east side of the roundabout is excellent black bear habitat. Choose a camp spot away from slough mouths and feeder streams.

Mile 585 (941.9 km): The Yukon River and Koyukuk village! There are two beaches in Koyukuk—one facing the Koyukuk River and another around the corner on the Yukon River. They are equally close to the center of town. The Yukon side beach is a little flatter and more open. There are no visitor facilities here, but there is a small store and post office. Koyukuk is frequently flooded and rebuilt, changing the town layout. Now, unless you are folding your boat into small packages to mail it, it is time to float the Yukon! You'll love the increased current, ease of finding firm campsites, and the steady breeze to hold the bugs down.

Ta da!

Kuskokwim River

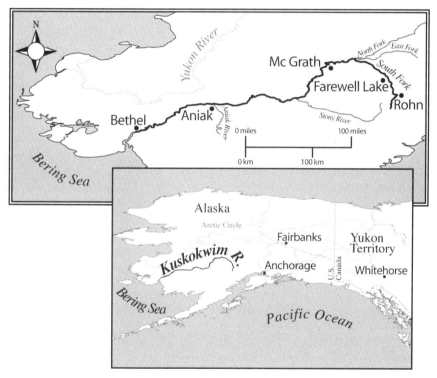

The Kuskokwim River, the second largest drainage in Alaska, is the oddball in this book: it is the only river not directly connected to the Yukon. But, the two channels share a delta plain and are separated by only 20 feet of elevation. The Kuskokwim and Yukon were probably tributaries in the geologic past. They are still connected by winter trails and cultural ties. Paddling the Kuskokwim offers the breadth of experience possible on the Yukon, but in a compressed period of space and time.

Unfortunately, the Kuskokwim is almost unknown outside Alaska. This is undeserved and probably because not a single road crosses the 600 miles of channel, reducing the number of people who encounter it. The river is a remote gem.

The Kuskokwim was not always so isolated. In fact, it was the first route into Interior Alaska for Russian explorers in the late 1700s. Russian Orthodox missionaries founded Kolmakof, one of the first European settlements on mainland Alaska, along the riverbank where the mountains meet the flat delta. Using it as a base, they spread out across the Interior and the delta. This history is reflected in the onion domes of the Russian Orthodox churches, the geographic center of many villages lining the lower banks today.

The rich people history is dependent on the natural bounty of the area. The thick salmon runs and abundant waterfowl, attracted by the fertile silt, swamps, and lakes, supported a relatively high population of people for thousands of years. Although communities have changed significantly over the last 200 years, the Kuskokwim River delta remains one of the most densely populated regions of Bush Alaska. Most villagers continue to practice some degree of a subsistence lifestyle.

Planning the Paddle

Introduction

The Kuskokwim River is the most difficult body of water to access in this book. Choices about where and how to begin and end the trip will ripple across gear options, boat type, and how long the bill lingers on the credit card.

There are three main sections of the Kuskokwim: the upper forks, the gentle, wide middle river, and the sprawling, tidally influenced delta. The upper forks are extremely remote, heavily braided, and rarely paddled. The middle river passes through mining country, passing a village roughly every other day. The delta feels almost densely populated as the Kuskokwim reluctantly meets the Bering Sea.

The South Fork is accessible only from small airplanes, landing on gravel strips or lakes. This swift, heavily braided channel rushing down

It doesn't take very high waves to force a canoe ashore, especially if they are following waves. The Kuskokwim River is wide, windy, and open. Expect to spend many days like this view, camping on shore waiting the weather out. Extra food and paperback books are essential camping gear.

from the Alaska Range is extremely remote and usually floated only during hunting season. (When I canoed into the village of Nikolai, a man, probably in his seventies, greeted me at the beach with the line, "I've never seen anyone do this river in the summer. And never in a boat so small.") *Floating the South Fork is only recommended for cautious paddlers with extensive experience on braided rivers.* There are many sweepers, the water is swift, the channel can be extremely difficult to follow, and the consequences of losing your boat are severe: there is nothing but swamp, forest, and mosquitoes to guide you to the next village. No one will come along to help you out. There are no options for pulling out; once you float past Farewell Landing, you have to complete the South Fork.

But this section also provides the best wildlife viewing on the Kuskokwim. There is a large buffalo herd, transplanted to the Farewell Lake area from Delta, Alaska in the 1960s. You will almost certainly encounter at least a few of these prairie monsters grazing the riverside willows. Besides that oddity, there is a relatively high concentration of the standard Alaska large mammals: moose, brown and black bears, and howling wolves.

About 20 miles past the village of Nikolai, the North Fork joins the flow, creating the main Kuskokwim. The main stem is a gentle, meandering paddle through low, forested hills. The banks are relatively densely populated by Alaska standards, passing a village at least every two days, sometimes much more frequently if you count the numerous small mining operations, lodges, and fishing camps. The most common route to paddle on the Kuskokwim is from McGrath to Aniak due to the excellent air cargo service between Anchorage and these Bush hubs, the relatively fast current, and the scenic, sheltering hills.

The tide can surge from the Bering Sea 150 miles upriver to Aniak, the first village after the river leaves the confining Kuskokwim Mountains. Between here and the mouth, the river sluggishly meanders across a nearly treeless plain. Wind can be vicious, and sea kayaks are probably the safest, most reliable boats. Canoeing is possible, but bring plenty of food, since you will certainly be camping for days at a time, waiting out weather.

The Yukon-Kuskokwim Delta has almost 50 villages clustered across the plain. On a sunny weekend day, the frequent skiff traffic can reach an annoying density as Bethel residents head to camps as far upstream as Napaimiut. However, boat drivers here are unusually courteous, and either swing wide to avoid swamping your boat with their wake or else pull alongside to talk. Paddlers are rare and people will be very curious about you.

Where does the Kuskokwim begin and end?

There are three forks: the North, South, and East. The North and East (sometimes called the Dry) Forks are quite narrow, short, and choked with sweepers and deadfall. They are relatively minor tributaries and should not be paddled.

The South Fork begins deep inside the Alaska Range, draining the north-facing glaciers into the Interior. Russian fur traders and missionaries crossed this pass from Cook Inlet to the Interior. They had terrible trouble with the upper rapids, and you will, too. It is recommended—and this guide assumes—that paddlers start no higher than Rohn Roadhouse, a point well downstream of all major rapids.

Most paddlers travel from McGrath to Aniak since the water is easy to float and these villages have excellent plane service. There are many villages and camps along the way, so, although wildlife sighting will probably be minimal, this section is a journey rich in human experience.

Almost no one paddles below Aniak. Bethel is the best village to leave from if you do. It is the last large village before the water becomes fully salty with the Bering Sea. It is possible to time the tides to get closer to the ocean, and then, more importantly, back to Bethel again. However, there is a subtle transition between river and sea with no real villages to bail out in if you get in trouble. Bethel, with multiple cargo and jet passenger flights a day, is a great spot to declare the end of the Kuskokwim.

Paddling Skills

The South Fork of the Kuskokwim is rated Class I-II but that does not reveal the difficulty. Below Rohn, the South Fork is swift and heavily braided as it rushes down the bench from the towering Alaska Range to the broad Interior valley. The water places a premium on route-picking skills; it is not the place to learn how to paddle braided channels. The river becomes particularly treacherous as its slope decreases and begins to cut a deeper, narrower channel around 25 miles above Nikolai. Here, many channels dead-end in snag piles. Some swiftwater cuts through spruce forests and is entirely blocked by sweepers; if you find yourself in one of these deadly stretches, there is no practical way to back out. *Do not travel the South Fork unless you are expert at paddling braided rivers.*

The main stem Kuskokwim River is entirely Class I. That does not mean it is easy to paddle. It is quite wide—up to a mile and a half on the delta—and just a breeze can churn the water into impassable waves.

Timing

A trip from Rohn Roadhouse on the South Fork to Bethel is a leisurely 4 to 5 week float. For a McGrath to Aniak paddle, budget around 10 to 14 days.

Season and weather conditions will dramatically affect the trip time. The river rises very quickly after heavy rains, with water speed picking up as well. And plan on being able to paddle only every other day below Aniak if you are in a canoe. If in a kayak, plan on camping every third day through here as a rough rule of thumb.

The ice is consistently gone on the entire floatable river by the beginning of June. Fall storms start on the delta by the beginning of August, and most paddlers should time their trips to avoid them. Winter quickly descends around the end of September or the beginning of October.

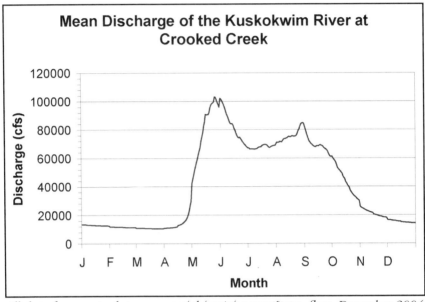

All data from waterdata.usgs.gov/ak/nwis/current?type=flow. December 2004

Boat Type

A sea kayak is the easiest boat to paddle from Nikolai to the Bering Sea. There are numerous villages along the way, so food restocking is very easy, overcoming the disadvantage of a kayak's small carrying capacity.

On the South Fork above Nikolai, sea kayaks are less useful. The channel is relatively narrow and wind is less of a concern. Instead, a canoe is handy since they are easy to get in and out of when you inevitably ground the boat on gravel bars, or, if you need to hop out in an emergency when smashing into a snag pile or hanging up in a sweeper. Some hunters do take catarafts down the South Fork. This is fine, but all boaters on the South Fork must be expert braided-stream navigators.

Weather and Water

The Interior is warm and mostly sunny during June and July. On the hottest summer days, the air can reach into the 80s, but the high 60s or low 70s are a more typical temperature. Thunderstorms tend to be quite cold and intense, but short lived. It can rain for weeks at a time, though. And when it does, watch out. The river rises very quickly after heavy rains. Be sure to pull all gear up to high ground at night, dragging it to a higher elevation, not just a long distance over flat gravel bars. The river can easily rise a foot while you are sleeping.

Beginning roughly around Sleetmute, the weather begins to feel more coastal, cooling and dampening considerably. A foggy drizzle can settle in for days, only to be dispersed by tremendous winds. Make sure you have a high-quality rain suit and plenty of warm, dry clothes for this section.

Drinking Water

Every inch of the Kuskokwim, including the South Fork, is heavily silted. Water filters will plug up almost instantly. You have to boil water and let the silt settle out overnight.

Gear

Getting the boat to the put-in and take out is both a challenge and the primary limiting factor of the trip. To paddle the South Fork, you will have to fly in with a chartered small plane. The choice of wheeled or floatplane determines boat type, beginning point, total gear weight, and overall cost of the trip.

Two operators (listed in the South Fork detailed description) fly canoes or kayaks as external loads on the plane floats. Besides costing a pile of money, flying in a hard-shell boat means the trip begins at Farewell Lake, the only upriver spot where you can land with floats. There is also an almost 1 mile portage from the lake down to the river.

Flying in on a wheel plane is considerably cheaper and more flexible in landing choices. However, you must have a folding boat, which is more problematic to paddle. Most wheeled planes will also have lower seating and cargo capacity than a floatplane.

As a last note, it is possible to fly in stove fuel on these planes since they are chartered and not a common carrier. But be sure to mention fuel in your discussion with the pilot when making a reservation.

The cheapest and easiest way to access the Kuskokwim is to fly your boat into McGrath on a regularly scheduled cargo flight from Anchorage. Besides being relatively inexpensive, cargo size is not a limiting factor and you can fly in whatever boat type you prefer. You will have to buy stove fuel after arriving, but that should not be a problem.

Leaving the Kuskokwim is relatively simple. Aniak has regularly scheduled cargo service. Bethel has almost daily flights of large cargo planes. There is a choice of at least three cargo carriers, so the taxi ride from the beach to the airport in Bethel might be more expensive than the freight charges back to Anchorage.

Maps

USGS 1:250,000
  McGrath
  Medfra
  Iditarod
  Sleetmute
  Russian Mission
  Bethel

Rest and Resupply Points

River Mile/km	Town & Zip Code	Road	Cargo Plane	Grocery Store	Café
69/111.1	Nikolai 99691				
95/153.0	Medfra No PO				
168/270.5	McGrath 99627		✓	✓	✓
308/496.0	Stony River 99557				
340/547.4	Sleetmute 99668				
347/558.7	Red Devil 99656				
457/735.8	Crooked Cr. 99575				
457/735.8	Aniak 99557		✓	✓	✓
488/785.7	Kalskag 99607•	•Upper & Lower Kalskag 99607 (Use just Kalskag, AK for address)			
536/863.0	Tuluksak 99679				
555/894.0	Akiak 99552				
567/912.9	Akiachak 99551				
597/961.2	Bethel 99559		✓	✓	✓

A Few Notes

While paddling, you will see many more communities than are listed here, particularly between Red Devil and Bethel, where there are numerous fish camps and older villages that are only lived in seasonally. These places don't have mail, public phones, or other services for travelers.

Bethel, with a population of nearly 6,000, is a small city in the Bush. After the quiet of the river, many paddlers will find the hubbub almost overwhelming. There is a choice of cargo and passenger airlines, grocery stores, numerous hotels, bed and breakfasts, restaurants (including franchised fast food), and taxis.

The South Fork

Miles: 168 miles (270.5 km) from Rohn Roadhouse to McGrath

Estimated Time: 5 days

Water Class/Hazards: Below Rohn Roadhouse, there are no rapids larger than a Class II riffle. However, the South Fork is a potentially lethal piece of water. There are numerous snag piles, sweepers, and the rare dead-end channel.
   Do not paddle this fork unless you are an expert at paddling braided rivers. Not only is the water difficult to figure out, no-one else will be on the river. If you get in trouble, you are on your own. There are no trails or roads to follow for help.

Access: Susitna Air Service
   Mile 76.5 Parks Highway
   Willow, AK
   (907)495-6789

   Willow Air Service
   Mile 70 Parks Highway
   Willow, AK
   (907) 495-6370 1-800-478-6370
   www.willowair.com

   Both of these plane operators have external load permits for carrying boats outside the plane on floats. Expect to pay through the nose for this unusual license. Also, be sure to be very specific in your conversation with the operators about boat type, gear, and number of passengers. This will greatly affect the number of trips, possible landing areas, and even whether or not you can fly in on their permit type at all.

Maps: USGS 1:250,000
   McGrath
   Medfra

Rest and Restocking: Nikolai and Medfra have extremely small stores, open rarely and erratically, with a spartan selection of non-perishable food. McGrath has a small but well-stocked store with an excellent choice of fresh fruit and vegetables.

Weather: Relatively warm and dry Interior weather, with sharp, sudden thunderstorms usually followed by cloudless days.

Section Description

The South Fork of the Kuskokwim River begins in the glaciers clinging to the Alaska Range. The melting ice carries silt, sand, and gravel in choking quantities down from the mountains, depositing it in heavy braids across the bench to Nikolai. This is swift, rocky, and occasionally tree-choked water.

All access to this fork is by air. There are two primary landing areas: a dirt strip at Rohn Roadhouse and a dirt strip or the water of Farewell Lake, on whose shore sits Farewell Lake Lodge. The strip at Rohn Roadhouse is right next to the river, and it is a relatively short haul to shore. Farewell Lake is set back about a mile from the bank of the South Fork, so you should budget time for a multiple-trip portage.

There is only one village, Nikolai, actually on the South Fork. So, for the purposes of clarity on the river, this section will cover down to McGrath, although that village is on the main-stem Kuskokwim.

As an interesting note, the Iditarod Trail roughly parallels and frequently crosses the river over this entire section. Rohn Roadhouse, Nikolai, and McGrath are official race checkpoints. The trail is an impassable swamp in the summer, but alert paddlers will occasionally spot flagging, markers, and dirt work along the route.

South Fork to Medfra

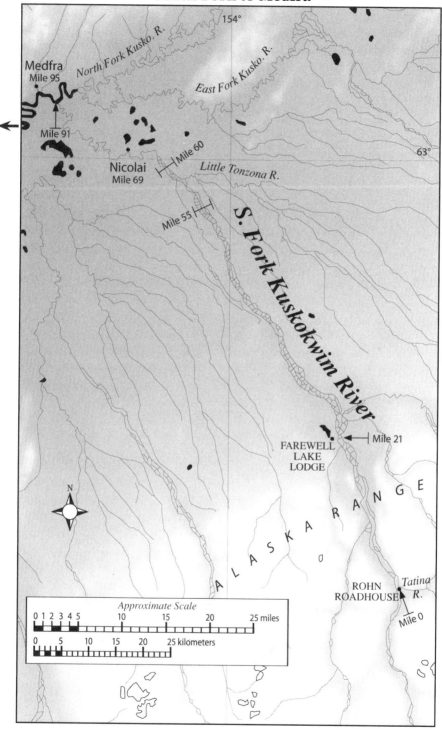

Medfra to McGrath

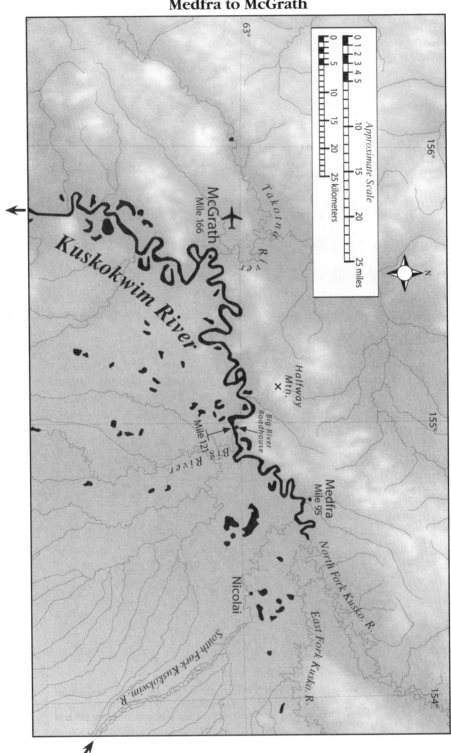

Significant Points

Mile 0: This guide begins at Rohn Roadhouse. The gravel landing strip and cabin sits at the junction of the Tatina River and the South Fork of the Kuskokwim. The scenery is mind blowing. The Alaska Range towers over the channel, and, on a clear day, you can see the heavily braided South Fork flowing off into the northern distance. There is a small cabin here, which serves as a checkpoint on the Iditarod Trail Sled dog race. I am unable to find any information on making arrangements for staying here, so do not expect to stop in the cabin.

The river is swift, gravelly, and rather shallow in places. This is a good introduction to the next few days paddling. The braids here are relatively easy to follow, the channels are relatively wide, and there are not many black spruce-lined cutbanks over the next 20 miles. That does not mean you don't have to concentrate on route picking; it just means this is a relatively easy warm-up for the more challenging water ahead.

Mile 21 (33.8 km): Farewell Lake Lodge Landing. If you are floating by on the river, it is unlikely you will see or notice the bare patch on the bank, but if you begin your trip here, you will become quite familiar with the spot as you make multiple trips hauling boats and gear.

This point also marks the beginning of the section where the buffalo roam. If you see a brown bear the size of a tank out of the corner of your eye, take a second look. That will be a buffalo grazing the banks, an odd sight indeed.

Over the next 20 miles or so, the river is heavily braided and the shore will become increasingly timbered.

Paddling Braided Rivers

As you paddle a braided river, try to pick the widest channel that holds to the middle of the river. It is always best to paddle with bare gravel bars on both banks. However, if given a choice between a channel lined with cottonwoods or one lined with black spruce, follow the cottonwood channel; eroding banks undercut black spruces, leaving them leaning across the water as sweepers. Cottonwoods and poplars have a much weaker root system and are more likely to wash away from the bank. Also, when you inevitably ground the boat on a shallow gravel bar, hop out on the upstream side. As you push the boat across the rocks, always keep a firm grip on it. And test the water depth before committing your foot to a forward step; the current frequently cuts bars off abruptly.

Mile 55 (88 km) (roughly): The topography begins to flatten and the river begins to cut a narrower, deeper channel. Wide, flat gravel bars become less common, and tree-lined cutbanks, snag piles, and narrow channels leading off through the woods become more prevalent. ***This is the most dangerous stretch of the river.*** Be cautious before committing yourself to a specific route. Hold back and maneuver to give a long view down the channel. Delay committing to a route as long as possible. Also, keep a sharp eye out for small channels ending in snag mounds. ***Be very paranoid about every route choice.***

Mile 60 (96.6 km): Phew! What a relief! The river now flows in a more conventional single channel. The current begins slowing, too, and the river takes meandering turns. For the first time, you may encounter motorized skiffs from the village of Nikolai cruising the river, cutting firewood or traveling to hunting camps.

Mile 69 (111.1 km): Nikolai. This community of 100 people is the only village on the South Fork. Founded at the head of large-boat navigation (as you can plainly tell, having traveled through what a large boat can't handle) by Athabaskan Indians and Russian missionaries, this is now one of the most isolated villages on the Kuskokwim. There is a small airstrip, and the Iditarod Sled Dog Race uses the village as a checkpoint. Visitor facilities are very limited—in fact, people will be very surprised to see a paddler. One elder drove his four-wheeler along the bank, taking pictures of me as I canoed away. You are the oddity here. The store is quite small and open sporadic hours. If you must have some item, you can ask around and probably get it opened. The city office is large, friendly, and well maintained.

Mile 91 (145.6 km): The North Fork joins the South Fork here to make the main Kuskokwim River. There are quite a few private fish camps scattered around the junction. Please respect the owner's privacy, although if they wave you over, they will be curious as to what you are doing.

The current slows considerably beginning a few bends past Nikolai, continuing until well past McGrath. The wind will be at your face, back, or, rarely, in the lee as the river bends through the contortions ahead. Depending on water level and wind direction, you will do well to paddle 30 miles in an eight-hour day. The water level can rise rapidly after heavy rains, so be sure to stack your boat and gear on higher ground overnight. Campsites are also considerably muddier and less frequent than on the South Fork. If you see a good spot but planned on paddling for another half hour, stop at the good spot; you are unlikely to find a better one soon.

Mile 95 (152 km): Medfra. The only indication from the river that this town of six people exists is the CONEX trailer and rusting mining equipment on the cutbank. It is inhabited by a few former workers at the shuttered Nixon Fork mine, and there are persistent rumors that the mine might restart and the town might grow again. In the meantime, there is an extremely small store and airstrip set back in the valley from the river and no visitor facilities.

Mile 121 (194.8 km): Big River Roadhouse. The sparse ruins sit on the bank opposite the Big River mouth. Nestled in the willows, alders, and mosquitoes, there are only a few logs and rusting cans to mark the former Bush hotel which operated when there was a regular dogsled trail through here in the winter. The relatively clear water of Big River can have excellent fishing, but you would have to travel a little upstream to find it.

Mile 166 (267.3 km): McGrath. The largest village in the Kuskokwim Interior is stretched along several bends of the river. The main beach is past the old log city office and is marked with a picnic table, a trash can or two, and a clear view of and access to the buildings of downtown. There are more visitor facilities here than in any other Interior village: large-plane cargo service, two bed and breakfasts, a choice of restaurants and bars, as well as a well stocked grocery with small bank and ATM. Camping on the beach or leaving your gear unattended is not recommended. If you need to camp in McGrath, pass the main beach and try to find an out of the way spot in the willows between the river and airstrip.

Kuskokwim River Guide

McGrath to Aniak

Miles: 289 miles (465.3 km)

Water Class: Class I

Estimated Time: 10 to 14 days

Access:
Pen Air (passenger and small cargo)
(800) 448-4226
www.penair.com

Hageland Aviation
(866) 239-0119
www.hageland.com

Northern Air Cargo (large cargo)
(800) 727-2141
www.nacargo.com

Rest and Restocking Facilities: McGrath has a fully stocked grocery store and two bed and breakfasts. Aniak is a relatively large village, with groceries, large plane cargo service, and a number of bed and breakfasts.

Maps: USGS 1:250,000
McGrath
Iditarod
Sleetmute
Russian Mission

Section Description

The Kuskokwim is a sluggish, winding river making its slow way through the largely unpopulated stretch of river from McGrath to Stony River. Downstream from this village, the river becomes almost cosmopolitan, passing a camp, old mine, active lodge, or village several times a day. River traffic picks up considerably, and barges will probably pass by once a day. Barges do not cause difficulty for paddlers since they are slow moving and follow the main channel.

After flowing through the Kuskokwim Hills, the last major barrier to reaching the sea, the Kuskokwim begins the sprawl across the Delta at Aniak. There is a fish camp next to almost every trickle of a creek flowing into the river between Crooked Creek and Aniak.

McGrath to Sleetmute

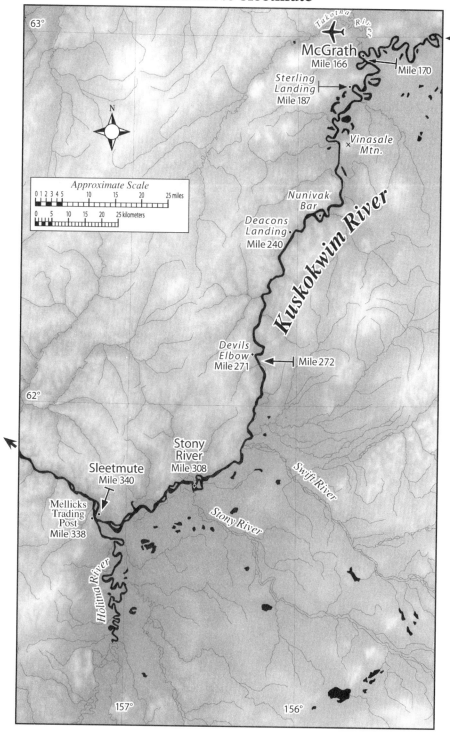

63°

Takotna River

N

McGrath
Mile 166

Mile 170

Sterling Landing
Mile 187

Vinasale Mtn.

Nunivak Bar

Deacons Landing
Mile 240

Kuskokwim River

Devils Elbow
Mile 271

Mile 272

62°

Stony River
Mile 308

Sleetmute
Mile 340

Swift River

Mellicks Trading Post
Mile 338

Stony River

Holitna River

Approximate Scale

0 1 2 3 4 5   10   15   20   25 miles

0   5   10   15   20   25 kilometers

157°

156°

Sleetmute to Aniak

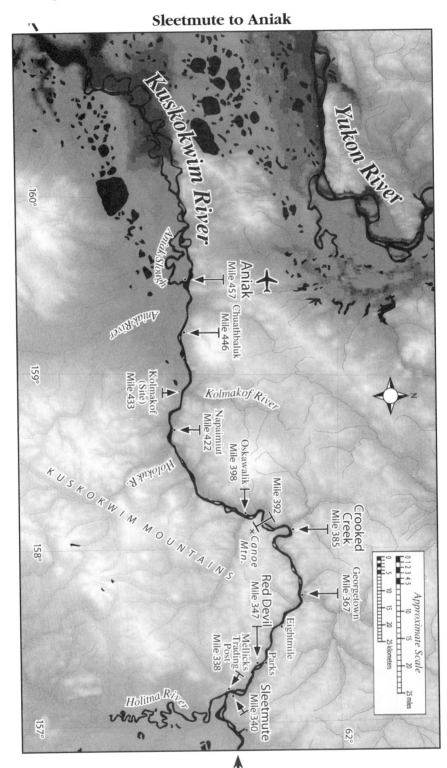

Significant Points

Mile 170 (273.7 km): The meander shown on the USGS map is now cut off and in the process of becoming a stranded oxbow. Take a sharp left and avoid the extra miles of travel.

Mile 187 (301.1 km): Sterling Landing. This clear spot in the riverbank is an unloading point for barges delivering machinery to mines in the Roundabout Mountains. There are no facilities here, just random heavy equipment, fuel drums, or the odd pickup truck. For the next 30 miles, the river meanders across flats. It feels like the current picks up a bit, although that is a subtle sensation.

Mile 240 (386.4 km): Deacon's Landing is a privately owned trapping camp.

Mile 271 (436.3 km): The Devil's Elbow has a small whirlpool and other odd, boiling currents as the river makes a sharp bend. The water should not pose any problem provided the weather and paddler are calm. If it is windy, however, you would be well advised to stick closely to the far right bank and be prepared to stop for a while and wait for more favorable conditions.

Mile 272 (437.9 km): There is a small complex of private cabins on the left bank, just past the point at Devil's Elbow, including a barge landing. The cabins shown on the USGS map on the right bank are

Below McGrath, barges are a common site. Unable to leave the main channel, they have the right of way. They do not throw much of a wake and do not cause paddlers problems.

no longer there. Past here, the river begins to pick up speed, and, with a favorable wind, it can be comfortable to paddle 40 miles a day between here and Stony River. The high hills on the right bank make for pleasant scenery and firm ground camps.

Mile 308 (495.5 km): Stony River. This very small village does not have visitor facilities. The 60 people live in a small collection of cabins just past the mouth of the Stony River. This village was a planned community built in 1960. Before then, families lived in camps up and down the river and had to send their children to boarding school. With the founding of Stony River, children could live with their parents and attend school locally.

This marks the rough border between the Interior Athabaskan Indians and coastal Yup'ik Eskimo, and many residents are a combination thereof. There are also a number of hunting and fishing lodges through here, and there is a steady outside presence in the summer.

Mile 338 (544.2 km): Mellick's Trading Post is a small compound of buildings set in a sheltering valley between two hills. Originally a busy store, this is now a private fishing and hunting lodge. The store figured prominently in the local area, and you will almost certainly hear the name mentioned.

Mile 340 (547.4 km): Sleetmute is a larger, more visitor-friendly village than Stony River. The city office, store, and post office are within a quick walk from the beach. An old Russian Orthodox church's onion

A gate blocks the road leading to shuttered Red Devil mercury mine.

dome marks the downstream border of the main village, but power lines go all the way downriver to Parks, serving scattered cabins and camps—the suburbs, if you like.

Sleetmute also marks the return of mountains lining both sides of the river. The Kuskokwim Hills are the last geographic barrier before the flat delta country. Weather will become gradually cooler and wetter. The current also slows considerably through this obstacle. Depending on wind speed and direction, paddlers will be doing well to paddle 20 to 25 miles in a day through these hills.

Mile 347 (558.7 km): Red Devil is an old mining town, serving as the base for workers at the Barometer Mine and others which worked the abundant mercury deposits in the western hills.

Mercury mining is no longer a viable business—for obvious reasons—but old mine buildings are in good shape and many are visible from the river. There is a barge landing and access road to one mine well before the village that is still used occasionally. Red Devil has minimal visitor facilities since most residents go to Sleetmute for services.

Mile 367 (590.9 km): Georgetown, a gold-mining boom town founded around 1900, is now a large, privately owned camp.

Mile 385 (619.9 km): Crooked Creek is a mining and Native village nestled in a protective bend in the river. Around 140 people lived here in 2000, and there is a city office and small store.

The Great Bend, the U-turn in front of the village, can be quite windy and tricky to paddle. Stick close to shore as you travel through here, and try to cross in the lee.

Mile 392 (631.1 km): Canoe Village, while marked on USGS maps, does not exist. The current begins to pick up slightly through here, and 25 to 30-mile days should be possible, wind and waves permitting.

Mile 398 (640.8 km): Beginning with Oskawalik, the riverbanks will be densely lined with seasonal fish camps. Skiff traffic begins to pick up considerably, too. Most of these camps are not marked on maps, and almost any clear-flowing creek will have a cabin next to it.

Mile 422 (679.4 km): Napaimiut used to be a year-round mining camp—hence the cemetery and two-story buildings. Now it is a summer fish camp, its residents spending the winter in larger villages. The village also marks the last of the Kuskokwim Hills. There will still be hills above the river, but only on one bank.

Napaimiut is a former village, and now used as a fish camp in summer.

Mile 433 (697.1 km): The site of Kolmakof, the first Russian fort on the Kuskokwim, is now only a mark on the map; nothing remains of the community across from the mouth of the Kolmakof River.

Mile 446 (718.1 km): Chuathbaluk is a satellite community of Aniak. Its residents tend to be more traditional than people in the larger, downriver community. There are no real visitor facilities here.

Mile 457 (735.8 km): The breakwater unmistakably marks the village of Aniak, the end of the trip for most Kuskokwim paddlers. This large village on the edge of the delta has regular plane service and a few bed and breakfasts. The village serves as a minor hub for flying wealthy anglers into lodges on the Aniak River for salmon and trout fishing.

Locally, the village marks the turnaround point for the Kuskokwim 300, a mid-distance sled dog race between here and Bethel. The second-largest purse in dogsled racing attracts the best mushers in the game, and the race is a midwinter institution on the Delta.

An ice road on the river connects Aniak with Bethel in the winter. Extreme tides can also be felt as far upriver as this point.

Aniak to Bethel

Miles: 140 miles (225.4 km)

Water Class: I

Estimated Time: 6 to 9 days, weather permitting

Access: Aniak and Bethel have some of the best air service in the Bush.
Alaska Airlines (service to Bethel)
(800) 252-7522
www.alaskaair.com

Pen Air (passenger and small cargo to Aniak)
(800) 448-4226
www.penair.com

Northern Air Cargo (large cargo Aniak and Bethel)
(800) 727-2141
www.nacargo.com

Rest and Restocking: Aniak, Upper Kalskag, Tuluksak, Akiak, and Akiachak all have village stores. Bethel has an enormous, well-stocked grocery store, and all other services, including a regional hospital, as well.

Maps: USGS 1:250,000
Russian Mission
Bethel

Section Description

The Kuskokwim Delta is one of the largest deltas in the world. The river is sluggish and wide as it spills over the plain. Some of the densest bird populations in North America nest in the abundant swamps and lake. Salmon runs are thick and fresh. The Delta has the densest population in Bush Alaska due to this fertile abundance. Paddlers will pass roughly a village a day, plus fish camps too numerous to mention or map. Skiff traffic is a constant buzz. And wind whips over the treeless plain, frequently churning the mile to mile-and-a-half channel into impassable waves. Paddlers should take enough food to camp unexpectedly, waiting the weather out. A sea kayak handles better in this water than a canoe.

Aniak to Bethel

Approximate Scale

0 1 2 3 4 5

0 5 10 15 20 25 Kilometers

5 10 15 20 25 miles

N

Bering Sea

Yukon River

Kuskokwim River

163°

162°

161°

160°

61°

Bethel
Mile 597

Kuregamut
Mile 589

Mile 590

Gweek R.

Kwethluk

Kwik

Kuskokuak Sl.

Akiachak
Mile 567

Akiak
Mile 555

Tuluksak
Mile 536

Mile 515

Lower
Kalskag

Palmiut Portage

Upper
Kalskag
Mile 488

Yukon-Kuskokportage

Mile 472-4

Mile 471

Mile 469

Aniak Slough

Aniak
Mile 457

The gray topographic scale is adjusted
to accommodate the flat delta. Mountains
are not as apparent as on upriver maps.

180

The delta channel is so wide it feels like the world is reduced to water and sky.

Significant Points

Mile 469 (755.1 km): The gravel bars downstream from Crow Village (a village marked on the USGS map, but there are no cabins remaining) are frequently the location of the Alaska Department of Fish and Game fish counting camp. There will be many freshly painted fish wheels, nets, overpowered skiffs, and a line of spanking new Weatherport tents lining the banks. This camp gathers data on the annual salmon runs, determining the timing and size of the assorted fish seasons. Not surprisingly, it also is the source of some resentment among locals.

Mile 471 (758.3 km): The industrial noise coming from the point on the left bank past the Fish and Game camp is the gravel pit for the city of Bethel. There will probably be at least a few barges, including one for crew quarters, tied up on shore. The delta becomes increasingly muddy—as you will notice for the next week as you try to find decent camps—and the Bethel road department has to travel more than 130 miles upriver to find enough gravel to meet its requirements.

Mile 472-4 (760.0-763.1 km): The gravel bars directly in front of the hills are the only dry ground, semi-private (provided you camp on the inside channel) camping spots until well past the Kalskag villages.

Mile 488 (785.7 km): Upper Kalskag. This Russian Orthodox Native village sits at the southern end of the Kalskag-Yukon portage, a winter trail over the swamps and lakes that separate the Yukon and Kuskokwim Rivers. Lower Kalskag is a Catholic village. The two communities split a number of decades ago over religious differences. If you need to use the phone or stop at the store, Upper

Kalskag has the closest, most direct route from the beach to the city office and store.

Depending on the weather, the wind will begin to feel noticeably stronger, churning bigger waves roughly around this point; there will no longer be hills on either bank. Prudent paddlers will want to stick reasonably close to shore, especially with any kind of breeze blowing, in case they need to make a quick hustle to safety. There are many fish camps along here, so if the wind does pick up and the waves are beginning to make you nervous, you will find many of the best spots are already taken and selection is limited.

A fine breakfast one month into a trip: salmon fresh from the smokehouse, cheese and Pilot Bread, a can of peaches and coffee. Life is good.

Mile 515 (829.2 km): The Shelter Cabin marked on the USGS map is now inaccessible from the river because of shifting mud bars.

Mile 536 (863.0 km): Tuluksak is a small Native village in a sheltering slough. You have to paddle against the current to reach this village, so only stop here in an extreme emergency. Tides routinely push as far upriver as Tuluksak. The channel between Tuluksak and Akiak is particularly wide and sluggish. There are few good campsites. Camp and wait before traveling this section if the wind and waves seem strong.

Mile 555 (893.6 km): Akiak is a relatively large village, extending to the next bend on the right bank. There are no longer any cabins on the left bank downriver, and the sandbar above the mouth of Kus-kokuak Slough is a popular recreational camping spot among locals. Skiff traffic between here and Bethel will be heavy.

Timing your travel to be on the river on the slack and ebb tides will speed up the paddling a bit. The tide rises and falls around a foot as a standard tide here, so it is time to begin to take water level into account when making camp for the evening.

It might be tempting to follow Kuskokuak Slough rather that the main channel. There probably isn't much difference in current speed between the two, and the slough can be shorter. However, shortcuts have a way of turning into longcuts. I have not paddled the slough and cannot recommend it.

Mile 567 (912.9 km): Akiachak is another large village, with many recently built houses, most of them brought in on barges. The site on a cutbank at the base of a U-shaped bend is good for fishing—in season, there will be lots of buoys on set nets to avoid—but the location is prone to flooding.

Mile 589 (948.3 km): There are many fish camps on both sides of the river along the bend near Kuregamut.

This barge sticks up from the bank on the cutoff to Bethel. Many more abandoned tugs and barges fill the alders. Besides being a tour of boating history, the area is also a clear illustration of how quickly the channel changes in the soft delta sediment.

Mile 590 (949.9 km): There are two sloughs that cut off the meander before Bethel. The first slough is more winding than the second, but is also much more sheltered (both sloughs are now wider than when the USGS map was made). The first slough has a high fish camp density. Be on the lookout for speeding skiffs coming around the bends. There is a barge and tug graveyard on the right bank just before the slough reenters the main channel, with many boats back in the alders. Besides being a fun tour through the history of boat manufacture, the area is a clear illustration of how quickly the channels shift; those boats floated to what is now dry ground.

Bethel barely appears on the horizon. Stick to the right bank to find the channel to the small boat harbor.

Mile 597 (961.2 km): Bethel! Welcome to the hub metropolis of western Alaska, population nearly 6,000. The port of Bethel covers the bank, with the commercial barge dock upriver, and the fuel barges and storage tanks farther down the bend. The ocean barges are stacked three containers high—or sometimes two containers and a full-size school bus. They are unloaded onto smaller, shallower draft barges here for the journey to upriver villages.

To reach the public boat launch, hug the right bank on the approach to the city. There is a small, protected channel leading away (right turn) from the barge docks. You can stash your gear in the alders on the opposite bank just after passing the No Wake buoy and park your boat on the opposite public beach if you wish. Just a few blocks toward town, there is a grocery store with a public phone to call a cab or truck to haul your gear from the beach. It is a several mile drive to the airport over busy roads with no sidewalks, so paying for the ride is a good investment. Also, you should not leave your boat unattended for very long, and certainly do not leave any gear unattended on the beach at all. Arriving early in the morning—as late as nine or ten—will considerably reduce the number of people out and about.

Getting a motel room in Bethel is both expensive and recommended. There are a number of cheaper, considerably more desperate looking motels along the waterfront, and one Motel 6 imitation with Hilton pricing more centrally located. There are no good camping places in town. If the timing works out that you will arrive on a weekend, you will probably be happier just camping on the river and timing your arrival for a Monday. It is possible to arrive in the morning, consign your gear to a cargo flight, and get on a passenger flight all in one day, but that would be a busy day indeed, and a harsh end to the trip.

Bethel is surprisingly cosmopolitan, attracting various people from all over the world. It is emerging as a regional hospital hub, and the population growth over the last ten years is mostly due to the expansion of the Yukon-Kuskokwim Health Corporation Hospital. There are also many other regional headquarters based here. And many Chinese-American-Italian and other odd combinations of restaurants that make a welcome end to camp food.

Bethel is a damp village (alcohol is legal to posses, but illegal to sell) surrounded by many dry villages. Many people come here to make up for lost time drinking, and there are depressing numbers of them staggering or slumped over on the roads. This should not cause problems for paddlers, but the observation is included here because the sight is so striking.

Bethel marks the end of the practical paddling on the Kuskokwim. It is possible to time the tides to reach saltier water, but Bethel basically marks the geographic end of the river. If you do go beyond Bethel, there are no more villages capable of flying out hard-shell boats—you either have to come back upriver or paddle along the Bering Sea to a larger community.

Ta da!

Bibliography

There are so many books about these rivers that a shorter bibliography is probably more useful than a longer one. This list distills the library of information available to some essentials. But, even among this refined group, some books are more equal than others, and one stands out in particular. Hudson Stuck's *Voyages on the Yukon and its Tributaries* is essential reading before leaving for any of these rivers. It is out of print, but is available for a high price through used book searches on the Internet and for free in Alaska libraries. The afternoons spent reading it will be well rewarded. For each river, one or two books are marked with a •. These are the books I would read before leaving for the river if forced to narrow the choices even further.

General Alaskana and River Travel

Ruppert, James. *Our Voices: Native Stories of Alaska and the Yukon*, University of Nebraska Press, 2001.

•Stuck, Hudson. *Voyages on the Yukon and its Tributaries*, Charles Scribner's Sons, New York, 1917.

Stuck, Hudson. *10,000 Miles by Dogsled*, Charles Scribner's Sons, New York, 1917.

Stuck, Hudson. *The Ascent of Denali*, Charles Scribner's Sons, New York, 1914.

Koyukuk River

Clark, Annette McFadyen. *Koyukuk River Culture*, National Museum of Canada, Ottowa, 1974.

Clark, Annette McFadyen. *Who Lived in this House?: A Study of Koyukuk River Semi-subterranean Houses*, Canadian Museum of Civilization, Hull, Quebec, 1996.

•Huntington, James as told to Elliott, Lawerence. *On the Edge of Nowhere*, Crown Publishers, New York, 1966.

Huntington, Sidney as told to Reardon, Jim. *Shadows on the Koyukuk*, Alaska Northwest Books, Seattle, WA, 1993.

•Marshall, Robert. Arctic Village, University of Alaska Press, Fairbanks, 1991 reprint.

Kuskokwim River
•Oswalt, Wendell H.. *Bashful No Longer*, University of Oklahoma Press, Norman, OK, 1990.

Porcupine River
• Josie, Edith. *Here are the News*, Clark, Irwin, and Co., Toronto, 1966.

Tanana River
Sturgis, Kent. *Four Generations on the Yukon*, Epicenter Press, Fairbanks, 1988.

Yukon River
Anderson, Barry. *Lifeline to the Yukon: A History of Yukon River Navigation*, Superior Publishing, Seattle, WA, 1983.

•Haskell, William. *Two Years in the Klondike and Alaskan Gold Fields 1896-1898*, University of Alaska Press, Anchorage, 1998.

Karper, Gus. *The Teslin River*, KUGH Enterprises, Whitehorse, YT, 1995.

Knutson, Arthur. *Sternwheels on the Yukon: How the Woodburners Won the North*, Knutson Enterprises, Kirkland, WA, 1979.

Madsen, Ken. *Paddling in the Yukon, A Guide to the Rivers*, Primrose Publishing, Whitehorse, YT, 1996. (good for approaches)

Parfit, Michael. *The Untamed Yukon River*, *National Geographic*, Volume 194, Number 1, July, 1998.

Rourke, Mike. *Pelly River*, Rivers North Publications, Houston, BC, 1995.

Rourke, Mike, *Teslin River, Johnson's Crossing to Carmacks*, Rivers North Publications, Houston, BC, 1995.

Rourke, Mike. *Yukon River, Marsh Lake, Yukon to Circle, Alaska*, Rivers North Publications, Houston, BC, 1985.

Saterfield, Archie. *Chilkoot Pass: The Most Famous Trail in the North*, Alaska Northwest Books, Anchorage, Seattle, & Portland, 1996.

•Schwatka, Frederick. *A Summer in Alaska in the 1880s*, Castle Books, Secauss, NJ, 1988 (reprint).

Yardley, Joyce. *Yukon Riverboat Days*, Hancock House, Surrey, BC, 1996.

Glossary

Braided river: A channel so choked with sand and gravel the river breaks into many fine strands. These are glacier fed rivers.

Brown bear: In Alaska, a grizzly bear.

Class I: Easy water. Fast moving water with riffles and small waves. Few obstructions, all obvious and easily missed with little training. Self-rescue is easy.

Class II: Novice. Straightforward rapids with wide, clear channels which are evident without scouting. Occasional maneuvering may be required, but rocks and medium-sized waves are easily missed by trained paddlers.

Class III: Intermediate. Rapids with moderate, irregular waves which may be difficult to avoid and which can swamp an open canoe. Complex maneuvers in fast water and good boat control in tight passages or around ledges is often required. Strong eddies and powerful currents can occur.

Cutbank: Steep, eroded side of the river. It is the frequently the outside bank of the meander and has a deeper channel then the inner, accretion bank.

Drift net: A free floating gill net, thrown from and accompanied by a skiff. Used for subsistence and commercial fishing.

Fetch: The length of uninterrupted water exposed to wind. Or, how much of a running start a wave has before hitting your boat.

Fish wheel: Rotating baskets set on a floating frame and anchored to shore. The current turns the baskets, which lift fish from the channel and drop them into a wet storage box. Used for subsistence fishing in muddy rivers.

Left bank: Right and left designations are always given from the downriver perspective.

Mileage: This is an elastic concept. Particularly on wide rivers, it possible to zigzag across the channel, turning what can be half a mile to a certain point into a four mile paddle. Mileage is given for a relative gauge, rather than a literal measurement.

Right bank: Right and left designations are always given from the downriver perspective.

Set net: A gill net tied at one end to shore and the other end is anchored in the water with a weight and marked with a buoy. Salmon migrating upstream on the back eddies are caught in the mesh and drown. Used for subsistence fishing.

Snag mound: A mound of driftwood trees, frequently at the point of a gravel bar, deposited at higher water.

Town: A community attached to the road system.

Village: A community not attached to the road system.

Index